EPISTULAE AD ECCLESIAS

(Letters to the Churches)

by

Rev. Ken D. Walston, Jr.

This book is the explicit expression and dedicated work of the author, who has been given by God an Outreach Ministry known as "Kenna Outreach".

The sole purpose in the publication of this book, is to give the reader insightful knowledge and revelation of what the Spirit of God is conveying through the author to enhance and encourage the reader in both Faith and Worship of the True and Living God (Yeshua ADONAI).

Softcover ISBN: 979-8-218-02017-0

PUBLISHED BY

SECTOR SEVEN
and
Ken-na Outreach Publications

 **Outreach Ministries** ®

www.kennaoutreach.org

Rev. Ken D. Walston, Jr. ✡
Executive Director of **Ken-na Outreach**™ Ministries ©1995
Ordained Minister and Doctor of Divinity

Printed in the United States of America

Table of Contents

Introduction

Epistulae ad Ecclesias (Letters to the Churches) is a compilation of teaching Revelations and Visions that the Lord has given explicitly through the author, in which he was told to write then down and send them out in what he calls (Letters). In the areas of the world where Ken-na Outreach has established fellowships with Believers in Christ called (Churches). These were written at different times from one another as they were inspired and have been sent out in order to inspire Faith and Hope and raise awareness in the Body of Christ of what the Lord God is choosing to share with The Believers of The Way.

Ken Walston started Ken-na Outreach in 1995 as a world-wide Evangelical Movement to the Body of Yeshua Adonai, (The Church) for the edification of ALL Believers who profess that YESHUA (Jesus the Christ) is their Lord and Saviour. The headliner for Ken-na Outreach is:

"Jesus is Lord and God!" Yeshua ADONAI

Ken had been a practicing Jew until 1981, when he received a physical manifestation and revelation from the Word of God, which convinced him beyond doubt that Jesus was the Messiah (*Yeshua HaMashiach*) and became Born Again (John 3:3-8); then called by the Lord to begin a Teaching Ministry.

1

And I show you a Mystery – Part I
(Absent from the Body)
(Written in April 2018)

This is the testimony of what God is giving through His imperfect servant, in order that what He has shown may be made a credible witness to His Majesty and Holiness.

The Lord God (ADONAI) has given me two great visions, one after the other, both of great significance and something that has been a mystery since the beginning of our human existence. As for myself, all of my life I have wondered what happens the moment after you die; and what was it like the moment God Created all things in Heaven.

This is the first vision that I received and went through. As I was worshiping and contemplating God and His Greatness, The Spirit of all Life opened before me a vision of Life after Death, and what each of our brethren who have fallen asleep in Yeshua (Jesus the Christ) are at right at this moment, in their Eternal Rest awaiting the Command, to be given by the Father, to the Son Yeshua, to go and get the Church; which is to resurrect the Dead in Yeshua first, and then we who are alive in Yeshua at that moment on earth, to be transformed from mortal into what is immortal, and be taken up to meet them in the Presence of the Almighty God. (1Corinthians15:51-53, 1Thessalonians 4:15-18)
It is unlike death for those who die without receiving the Free Gift of Salvation from God. For them, there is

another pathway they travel, and it is to the Grave and Death (Sheol); to a place of Darkness and Cold, separation from God and in Torment because of that separation, which they freely chose.

The Spirit allowed me to briefly witness what awaits those who Sleep in Yeshua. It is the State of Death where Eternal Life begins and Transends our physical mortality and where sin goes to the grave and dies with the body.

I was taken out of my body and transfigured into a state of Pure Energy (Spirit) and weightlessness. At that moment of being taken out of my body, I breathed in for the first time what felt like pure serenity, Life beyond anything experienced in my human being. It felt like being set free from the compression inside a shell, this Body, which is holding the life-force inside of it, keeping it alive. Once this Life Force is released from this Body, it feels like it expands beyond the space and time of this universe in Timeless Eternity.

All that was before me appeared to be in a cocoon of surrounding Heavenly Light (not sunlight like on earth), but a bright blueish glowing Presence of Light which Radiated in all directions to where I could not see anything but the Light surrounding me. There was no one else around me or with me, I was alone in the Presence of Absolute Power and Serenity, in an Eternal State of Being with no reality other than my Eternal Existence; no passing of time, and I had no remembrance of my earthly human life, no feelings of being in a physical body, only what surrounded me, Eternity.

Coming from the center of this surrounding Cocoon of Light was a Brighter, more intense Point of Light. I could tell that the surrounding Light around me was the Afterglow and Fluorescence of this one Brilliant Point of Light. I was completely engaged into that Point of Light and was prepared to stay there forever. I could feel absolute Love and Peace within me and surrounding me like a blanket. I had absolutely no desire to do anything but engage the Light and receive the Energy, Peace and Love coming from it. It was complete in its entirety, it is a State of Euphoric Bliss, a sanctuary of Eternal Peace and it is what awaits every Believer of Yeshua after they leave their mortal body behind. It is the definition of what is proclaimed as, "Absent from the body, present with ADONAI"; the Sleep that the Apostle Paul mentioned after this life ends. It is the Eternal Presence of God, holding onto you and keeping you Still. *"Be Still and know that IAM God"* (Psalm 46:10); actually, the translation means, "Absent from the body, in the Presence of ADONAI".

This is what it is, you leave the confines of the mortal cocoon (Physical Body) and the physical universe and are lifted out into a State of Spirit, that part of you which is the Life Force (Energy) within the Physical Body (the Real You). All of the frailty of the human experience you knew on earth is gone; all fear, all body pain, all temptations, all physical anxieties, all doubt, all memory, all hunger and thirst, all the people you knew, all family, everything that was human and everything that was corruptible.

Those who die (sleep) in Yeshua are literally in a State of Spirit, waiting for the moment when they shall be risen from being in Spirit (Sleep) and transfigured into an Eternal Physical Being (with a New Body) which is incorruptible (Lives Forever) in the Abode of Heaven which Yeshua has prepared for us. You do not go back into your human physical body but are resurrected into a New Physical Form which is Body and Spirit combined which lives in the Presence of God and Eternity; and you receive a New Name, a totally New Identity.

This waiting state of sleep is not sleep like in your earthly body where you are unconscious, out of reality and vulnerable while under the influence of sleeping. Human sleep is to rejuvenate the sinful human flesh, where this death sleep is a release of the sinful human flesh and all of the attributes associated with it. You become more brilliantly awake and aware of your existence than you ever could in your human state of being.

There is no awareness of time or the passing of time, time is for the mortal, within the confines of this physical universe and under the Laws of this physical universe. This is now a State of Immortality and under the Order of Eternity which to us is in the realm of the Supernatural and not confined to the Laws of this physical universe.
The Spirit reminded me of what He has said before, "You are Spirit Beings having a Human Experience."

This State of Rest or Spirit Being is not confined to anything, you are separated from your previous physical existence (bondage to a physical body) and free beyond anything you could ever imagine. You literally have the Mind of Yeshua and are sharing in all of the Virtues of God. There is absolutely no remembrance of the life you had as a physical Human Being at all; no hindsight only Pure Foresight as you are confronted with the Full Essence of God in Spirit and Power and are in His Everlasting Presence. He is holding you up, holding on to you, you are completely surrounded by His Safety and Protective Love.

The people who died in Yeshua 2000 years ago, or a thousand years ago, or 500 years ago, or fifty years ago, or just a moment ago, are all in the same State of Spirit Being or Rest as if they had just woken up and entered into the Presence of the Lord. You can feel yourself leaving this physical state of human being; pulled out and gladly leaving it all behind. No matter how good you lived or how happy you were in your physical human being, you can feel the death of it leaving you as you enter into a state of Spirit Being which surpasses all previous existence, and with it goes ALL of the memory associated with that previous human existence.

There is no concept of time or how many years have passed; it all just happened for each and every one of them a moment ago. The next moment for them, no matter how many days, weeks, months or years it is from now, will be when they (The Dead in Yeshua), are risen (Changed) from their State of Spirit (Rest) and joined to a New Form (Body); and then we who are alive in Yeshua on this earth, hear the Command of God, *"COME UP HERE!"* and we are changed from Mortal into Immortal (a New Form Body), and we meet them in the air. Then the entire Body of Yeshua (the

Church) will be Assembled before ADONAI Physically, not in Spirit, but in a New Physical Form; and so, Shall We Always be with ADONAI.

"For God so Loved the World, that He gave His Only Begotten Son, so that whoever believes in Him shall not perish [Die the Second Death] but receive Eternal Life."
(John 3:16)

These are not just some beautiful words or a romantic sentence to inspire the individual reading it, this is an Eternal Event, one that set the precedence for our Second Birth in Yeshua (Born Again) and assures us of our Eternal Life; but you must receive it, it is freely given by God, but assured in receiving it only through Faith...Faith in Yeshua! (Jesus the Christ).

2

And I show you a Mystery – Part II
(At the Moment of Creation)
(Written in April 2018)

This now, is the testimony of what ADONAI is giving through His imperfect servant, in order that what He has shown may be made a credible witness to His Majesty and Holiness.

ADONAI has given me two great visions, one after the other, both of great significance and something that has been a mystery since the beginning of our human existence. What was it like the moment ELOHIM Created all things in Heaven.

This is now the second vision that I received and how ADONAI actually allowed me to witness and participate through it. As I was worshiping and giving my daily dedication to Yeshua ADONAI, the Overwhelming Presence of ELOHIM suddenly was around me. Then suddenly, The Spirit of All Life brought me into His Presence, which was Pure Light with no substance; the Glory of what ELOHIM is and has always been and continues to be. Absolutely no physical presence of anything, even I was transfigured from the physical, into Pure Energy (Spirit).

What I was witnessing, existing in, looked like a one-dimensional surface of Pure Brilliance. There was a resonance, the Resulting Sound of ELOHIM, Pure and Radiant, Holy and Good; there was nothing but Brilliance, like white shining diamonds glistening with a sound coming from all directions, the Harmonic of ELOHIM that no creature had ever heard yet, because Creation itself had not occurred yet. It was the moment before the Beginning of All Things in Heaven were Created, Pure and Virgin, it was the Presence of ELOHIM in His Glory, within Himself – Omnipresent.

Then, out of the Presence of the Almighty, the entire foreground of vision ripped apart, and ELOHIM the Creator spewed forth what looked like Shafts of Brilliant Light, billions, and billions of them. They seemed to reach out into this one-dimensional plane to infinity. Then the entire surface moved outward in all directions as if creating a three-dimensional sphere, which then surrounded a Center Point of Brilliance, much Brighter than the surrounding radiance, which became The Throne of ELOHIM. It seemed like they all just hovered in place glistening with Radiance and a sound that had the appearance of the same harmonic as that which was coming from the Presence of the Almighty. Then a Tremendous and Raging Sound bellowed out from each Shaft of Light and brought forth Angelic Beings, Creatures of Substance of Light, Holy and Pure, Screaming into their existence Praises unto the Holiness of the Almighty God.

It sounded like a Roaring Thunderous Choir, Massive and Mighty, screaming in unison what sounded like **"Hallelujah!"**, long and sustaining with no end or break in between as if the sound was coming from their bodies bellowing outward. They were standing, leaping, flying, moving in all directions Rejoicing. As I was watching at the moment it occurred, I was caught up in the midst of the Thunderous Choir and began

Screaming to the top of my lungs in a manner that was not human. I was beyond my physical human capability in sound and hearing and in performance of my anatomic being. Nevertheless, there was massive strength and stamina through the course of time I was allowed to participate in this Glorious Event.

Just as this was occurring, it ended without warning or slowing, and I was made conscience again in my physical body. For a brief moment as I was coming out of this event, transforming from spirit back into my physical body I could hear myself Screaming from the Event and could feel my body falling fast and giving into extreme physical stress like I was about to have a heart attack and filled with complete exhaustion beyond any exercise I had ever been physically put through. As I battled to catch my breath, I began weeping and Praising ADONAI, for I knew that what the Ruach HaKodesh (Holy Spirit) had just shown me and allowed me to participate in, I believe no man has ever in this manner before.

As with other such visions that ADONAI has given me or allowed me to participate in, the Spirit instructed me to write this down and give it to the Body of Yeshua, my brethren. I have waited a month contemplating and praying over it. I have been afraid to even begin trying to explain what ADONAI bestowed upon me, that I may somehow distort the vision into something that I could receive credit for or give a false account of it because of my human frailty. All of this vision was something that is beyond our human comprehension and my ability to recant any of the actual feelings or substance of the Glory of ELOHIM connected to it. It was given to me as a man standing from a distance watching and then all of a sudden, I was in the midst of it participating. I witnessed and saw what I believe it was like and still is, before The Almighty Who Created all things in Heaven, when the substance of Being was within the all-Inclusive Being of the Eternal; and I felt as a Being Created out of the Spirit, what God perpetrates from His Holiness. As Sons of ELOHIM, through Yeshua HaMashiach, we are given All Things in Knowledge and Wisdom the Mystery of ELOHIM's Purpose to those who love Him.

To Yeshua ADONAI be the Glory and Honour, Praise and Worship from His creatures on earth, just as it is being done from the beginning of Creation in Heaven to this very moment. Amen!

"Let the heavens rejoice, let the earth be glad; let them say among the nations, "ADONAI reigns!"
(1 Chronicles 16:31)

3

The Mystery of God
(Written in May 1999)

Shalom… Baruch Hashem, Adonai
(Peace… Blessed be the name of the Lord God)

From Ken, who is an Elder in the Church, and who by Faith has been called by the Great God and Saviour, Jesus (*Yeshua ADONAI*) the Messiah (*HaMashiach*), to be a Believer and Teacher for the edification of the Believers of the Way, the Church, or Body of Messiah. May God the Father bring you Peace and Blessing according to your Faith…*Amen.*

To all of you who are in Jesus the Messiah, do you understand how blessed you really are?
Do you really understand that!

The Lord Himself has given you a NEW Name, an Everlasting Name…one that will live forever in the Book of the Living. God Himself has written your name in His Book, the Book of the Living, and NO ONE, not even God will remove it. For the Lord Himself has given that promise to us and taken a vow unto His own Name and fulfilled the promise by sealing it with His own blood. Once you received Jesus the Messiah in your heart as your Lord and Saviour a supernatural transformation took place in the spirit realm immediately. In the Presence of the Almighty God, ALL of Heaven rejoiced because you came into the Kingdom of God by way of your Faith in Yeshua the Messiah, and with that God the Father was glorified in the Highest. The Son of God,

Yeshua the Messiah, at that moment gave you a rebirth in the spirit and assigned you a NEW Name...and sitting at the Right Hand of the Father, He ordered His angel to scribe your name into the Lambs Book of the Living, and thus fulfilled the promise that "*where I go, there also shall you be*", and "*we shall reign in the house of the Lord forever*".

Now, the mystery in all of this is that even though we live in these bodies on earth and exist in this physical world, we also reside in spirit before the Lord. The Lord says that God cannot gaze upon sin and has no communion with the dead, yet even though our physical bodies have sin in them and the wages of that sin is death to our physical bodies, God has communion with us in the spirit through our rebirth with Jesus the Messiah and walks with us, and gazes upon us through the Blood of His Sacrifice and has made an Eternal Covenant with us through our <u>Faith</u> in Yeshua the Messiah.

Why then does God plead with us not to sin. It is because we have inherited sin in our flesh and are first born into that. The flesh and the sin in the flesh is man's true nature and it is opposed to God and His nature, for God is Spirit and Eternal and has created man in His Own Image, which is Spirit and Eternal, therefore every human being is truly made in the image of God by having imparted in them a Spirit which is Eternal

Now, the mystery in all of this is when the outer shell of the person (flesh) dies because of the inherited sin in it, the inner being (Spirit) will continue to live on in the realm of the Spirit (Eternal). If the person dies in their sin, meaning that they did not receive their Salvation and Eternal Life through Yeshua the Messiah by Faith, then this Eternal Spirit goes to the grave (*SHEOL-the first death*) and waits for the day of God's Judgment. On that day, God will command their Spirit out of the grave, and they will stand before the Almighty and be Judged according to what they have done against the Eternal Standard that God had set forth through the Law. The Law was never meant to save anyone from their sin. It was given by God to show where man fell short of righteousness with God because of sin. God imposed the Law in order to give man a standard for guidance which points towards God's Righteousness; but because the Law dealt with sin and its innate nature associated with the human heart, God Himself had to stand in proxy for man in order to reconcile man back to His Righteousness and Holy Presence.

Now, the mystery in all of this is that Yeshua the Messiah was the physical evidence of the unseen God...that He was one with the Father (one in the same). That the unseen God (Eternal Spirit) had made Himself visible to His Creation for the sole purpose of bringing them back unto Himself and forever transforming mankind from a state of sin, into a state of righteousness through Faith in Himself (Jesus the Christ).

The power that God has given us is complete control of this flesh and the sins of the flesh through His Word (Jesus the Christ), and our Faith in His Word.

Remember, Faith comes by hearing, and hearing by the Word of God. The Faith that I am speaking of is that which the Holy Spirit gives in truth through God's Spirit and we believe in it. It is not the faith that man acquires by his own understanding, experience and knowledge from the world through his flesh (self-sustaining mind and ego). Real and absolute truth comes through God's Spirit to our spirit because we have been given the Holy Spirit (Ruach HaKodesh), who resides in us once we receive Jesus the Christ, and the Ruach HaKodesh reveals all the mystery of God and the secret truths, which come from God the Father, through the Son and to every Believer. Therefore, what can we now say about all who have not received Yeshua Adonai (the Lord) …that their means to receive and apply truth is not within them because their faith is not based on truth but is based on what this physical world and their physical bodies can understand and apply in accordance with the five (5) physical senses and human logic.

Remember that God has an adversary in both the spirit and physical realm…in both the heavens and on earth. This adversary is OUR enemy, and its agenda is to completely upset, confuse and destroy our Faith in Jesus the Messiah. Its purpose is to deceive, lie and give false testimony so that mankind will not believe in Jesus the Messiah and therefore rob mankind of their only means salvation. Yeshua called this adversary Satan (or in Hebrew "Abaddon"), which means "Destroyer". Satan has no love for God and had sworn vengeance (Sealed Forever) against God and all of His creation especially against that which God had created in His Own Image…<u>Mankind</u>.

Now, the mystery in all of this is that God first created living beings within the environment of His Abode (Heaven), which is in the Spirit (Eternal). These beings had presence with the Almighty without restriction and innate characteristics of power and authority given as supernatural beings. Lucifer, whose name meant "Bringing Light", (later referred to by Jesus as Satan) was created at a supreme level as the Anointed Cherub. He was the one who guarded the Throne of God. He was revered as the most beautiful of heavenly beings. Embedded within his being were musical instruments, which gave sounds that were pleasing to God, and which gave great praise to the Almighty with every move he made.

Now, the mystery in all of this is that none of the heavenly beings that God had created were created in His Own Image…they were all free spirits who served God through His purpose. Even though God created Lucifer with great beauty, status, and purpose, and set him above the highest order amongst the heavenly hosts, Lucifer had an internal desire to aspire beyond his created status and to become like God…even to the extent of overthrowing God's Throne. As his desires became more and more intense and perverted, his created purpose became opposed to the Will in which God had created him for. Deep in Lucifer's being was a prideful arrogance and disobedience, which motivated him into rebellion against God. His great status and self-reverence inspired others of the heavenly hosts to side in with his desires which corrupted one third of all the angels and motivated them to stand with him in rebelling against God. The Lord God cast Lucifer and the rebellion of angels out of the Highest Heaven (away from the Presence of The Almighty and His Abode) and into an inner sanctuary of darkness which would later become the physical universe. Lucifer had now become the Adversary of God and stripped of his place and status with God and His Abode. As the Lord God cast Lucifer out of His Presence, He also transformed his being and all of the angels who followed him, into dark and deformed creatures of demonic order. With this came a metamorphosis of their spirit being and their names. Each were opposed to the Righteous and Holiness of God and His Order and each possessed a unique demonic identity and insurgent power. As they changed from Light into creatures of darkness, a shroud of deception and lies became their ambiance. Their witness was to defame and insult the Lord God and the Holiness of His Abode...to curse His Name and all of the Heavenly Hosts. They could never again turn back to God, nor go back to God or be restored to God...their fate was sealed in Eternal Damnation and their final Eternal Destination, the Lake of Fire, which was created for Satan and his fallen angels.

Now, the mystery in all of this is that since the Lord God had created all of the heavens and physical universe out of Himself, He could not simply destroy and send it into oblivion when He found displeasure in it. There is an order to what God has commanded forth, and a Holiness which is revered to Himself through it. Because God the Father is Eternal in all things, He has vision into what He will set forth in the future, this coincides with His Will…the Lord says, "*Nothing returns to Me void, all things are fulfilled*". This demonstrates His complete Sovereign Power and Authority over everything in Heaven, the physical universe, and on Earth (including, the Under World). God set into existence His Creation through His Word, in a Command which is still going forth to this day. All things were created through Him (The Word), and not one thing in all of creation was created without Him (The Word). The Word is of course, the Word of God (Jesus the Messiah). When God determined man's existence, He did so with the compassion and love as a Father would towards His children. We (human beings) were created in His image, for God said to us that "*you are god's*". Through man, God had personification and communion with His creation through Himself. Where the angels and the Hosts of Heaven proclaim "Holy, Holy, Holy is the Lord", only man proclaims "<u>Father</u>, you are Holy!". This distinct difference is what enraged Satan and the powers of darkness to set a course of vengeance towards mankind in order to defeat and humiliate God with what He now called His children.

When the Lord God created Lucifer, He did so as a servant but when the Lord God created Adam, He did so as a son. Adam was created by God's own hand from the dust (ground material) of the Earth. God molded his form into an image that would appear as God in the Flesh. Then the Lord God breathed his Life-Giving breath into the man, and he became a Living Being. Unlike the angels and Hosts of Heaven who appeared out of nothing as shafts of light and sound to begin their endless worship and praise, man was set apart at the next highest order, to one day sit at the Right Hand of God the Son (Yeshua HaMashiach), and rule over the nations of the Earth and be the judge of the Heavenly Hosts.

Now, the mystery in all of this is that God gave all of His creation a free and willful character. He gave all of His creation the ability of <u>choice</u>. God set before His creation the knowledge and value of Good and Evil. When rebellion broke out in Heaven, God judged according to the knowledge and value of Good and Evil with the Heavenly Hosts, and His judgment determined the Everlasting outcome of creation in that realm. With that judgment came a new order for all who rebelled and for all who were Faithful unto God, as well as a separation of the knowledge and value of Good and Evil. God Himself has chosen the balance for creation to be set with the knowledge and value of Good and Evil, yet in the Heavenly Abode of God, He has chosen to preponderate His own Nature and Will towards only Good. The value of Good in the nature of God is Eternal and Everlasting and shown to His creation in the virtues of Love, Mercy, Forgiveness, Peace and Grace which He expresses in ways that far exceed our human understanding or ability to express in such abundance as God is able to produce. The very essence and nature of God express these virtues so greatly that none other can be conceived nor portrayed by God Himself.

Now, the mystery in all of this is why has God chosen to expose man and the physical creation to the knowledge and value of Good and Evil in the first place...Why didn't God just place mankind in a perfect "Good" environment from conception? The dark void that God cast Satan into after his rebellion was the expanse of the physical universe before God had commanded Light and His Presence to appear. Everything was without form or substance; it was a holding place for the angelic beings who had defied and blasphemed God...a curtain between that which God sanctified (Good) and rejected (Evil). God created the physical universe as an expression of His Abode but reflective of the knowledge and value of Good and Evil, and in an environment where both Good and Evil could exist, and the Perfect Will of God could be demonstrated. Therefore, the physical universe would have and contain the knowledge, value, and substance of Good and Evil in every aspect of its creation. Thus, the Lord God Commanded, "*Let Light Be*" (*Yehi 'Or*) and all things physical in this universe began their creation. As part of the command in which God had set forth through "The Word" in creating the physical universe, came a displacement of Eternal substance into physical matter and energy. The Abode of Heaven where God reigns is Eternal (no beginning and no end) and Everlasting (perpetual in existence and no decay of substance), whereas in the physical universe God has chosen to divide the Eternal and Everlasting into phases and segments called "Time". He has chosen to regulate the phases and segments by equal intervals of calculated measure He called "Days". Nothing in the Abode of God (Heaven) has any measure of time which is relative to

24

the physical universe and its creation…as the Lord God says in reference to our existence here on Earth verses the equivalent measure as viewed in the Eyes of God in His Abode, "*a thousand years is but a twinkling of the eye*".

Now, the mystery in all of this is that the Lord God had chosen a central point in the physical universe to measure time, in both a "Coming and Going" and "Point to Point" relationship. When the Lord God referenced "*When God began to create Heaven and Earth*" (Genesis 1:1), He was making a distinct identity between all things created in the physical universe (heaven) and a unique place within it (Earth). The earth was formed as the central point where the Lord God would establish His physical presence in the universe and through His Virtue allow physical life to sustain itself. Therefore, God had proclaimed the Earth to be an extension of His Abode, and in plain view of the powers of darkness, who had been cast into the expanse which would become the physical universe, He announced the Earth to be His Footstool. The imagery being portrayed, is as the Lord God sits on His Throne in Heaven (Eternal), His Majesty (Dominance) extends to the physical creation through the Earth. About this the Lord God has proclaimed, "*On the Day of Judgment no one will be able to say that they did not know the existence of God, for nature itself proclaims God's existence, and the Earth is proof of His handiwork*". The absolute proclamation that the Lord God was making is that ALL physical life, the existence of life, and the Communion between God and the physical creation would be bound to this one central point within the entire physical universe…the Earth.

In the Divine Will of God, He commanded creation into existence, He also established the Order associated to sustaining the substance of matter and energy outside the Abode of Heaven and His Physical Presence (Eternal and Everlasting). This Order was given to creation in the form of physical laws we call Physics. The Laws of Physics apply themselves consistently throughout the physical universe and are proven by means of science. Science is the human interpretation of what man can deduce of the physical universe through applied and systematized knowledge. It uses what God has provided in the form of substance (matter and energy) and divides it into equitable conditions and conclusions based on scientific theory and physical evidence.

Now, the mystery in all of this is that what is unseen (God), has created all which can be seen (physical universe), and that man can only prove the existence of what can be seen through science, yet God is above everything in both existence and form and can only be accessed and recognized by man through Faith, because God is Supernatural. God is motivated by our Faith… *Faith without doubt.* So, when the Lord God created all things, He did so with "The Word" through a Command of Faith *without any doubt*, meaning that His Desire and His Will were set on one and the same thing, thus the Command was Faithful in both execution and fulfillment.

Why is *Doubt* such an important factor in relationship to Faith. . . Because the Order in which God has commanded the evidence of everything into being is through Faith. Quite simply, in the Eyes of God, *Doubt* is sin and in the Presence of God it is separation. It is the opposite of Faith and in opposition to the Nature and Will of God. *Doubt* opposes any action which is motivated by Faith, and in the realm of the physical world has an influence of a demonic spirit which denies and dilutes what Faith is calling forth. *Doubt* causes any request from the heart or desire for fulfillment to wait upon conditions which are satisfied either to physical laws or human understanding....it does not allow the request or desire to move into the realm of the unseen or supernatural (Spirit) where God exists and is motivated in exercising His Power and Authority. God is motivated by Faith, and Faith alone...this is the Divine Will of God!

Therefore, I charge you by the Name, which is above ALL names (Yeshua Adonai, Jesus the Christ), to request ALL things, every desire from your heart which is set on goodness, to be exercised in Faith which has *no doubt*, and to be steadfast, standing upon this Faith as a sure foundation. To call upon the Name of the Lord when *doubt* starts to set in, and the enemy of God comes against you. Remind the Lord of His promise (for God is not a liar and keeps His promises), that everything we ask for in His Name under agreement (in Faith *without doubt*) SHALL be given to us in order to glorify God the Father (John14:12-14)...*Amen*! Be as relentless in not giving up as our enemy is...for the Devil (Satan) who is spirit (part of the unseen) has great power and authority in this world (the realm of the physical universe) and knows that he has but a short time left. The Lord God had originally given this power to Man (Adam) but Adam fell into sin through his disobedience and blasphemy by not fulfilling the Command of God, which was for him to restrain from taking of the fruit from the Tree of Knowledge of 'Good and Evil'. At this time in man's existence, he was sinless in the Eyes of God and had been given ALL authority over the entire physical universe which was stationed for him on the Earth. Adam was commanded by God to subdue the Earth and all things within it. Satan and a third of the angelic hosts (who had been cast out of the Presence of God), were loose but in bondage within the void of the physical universe. When God created the control point for the physical universe where He would establish His Presence in it (the Earth), Satan and his hordes made a beeline to where that action was taking place. The powers of darkness had existence in the void for an Eon (uncalculated amount of time) before the Lord God set His Presence in Light upon the dark void and moved over the face of the waters of planet Earth. It was a beacon for the demonic beings to gravitate towards. As God fulfilled His purpose in creating the Earth, and the abode above it, the powers of darkness hid in the void of darkness around the Earth until the Lord God had finished his work. Then Satan in all of his arrogance and defiance made his presence upon the Earth but did not understand the meaning of God's purpose behind it. He was deceived in understanding the similarity that God had made between Heaven and the area called Paradise. He did not understand the purpose nor the meaning of the physical sun and the moon nor the billions of stars and lights in the sky; but when he saw Man (Adam), he knew exactly who he was, and he felt the Presence of the Lord God through the Man. The powers of darkness were unable to touch or disrupt the course in which God was taking the Man. God had given all of His Sovereign Authority to the Man within the physical universe and was preparing the Man to rule on His behalf. Before Lucifer was cast out of Heaven, he had gazed upon the Heart of God and saw what the Lord God had in way of the future, in line with His Will. He saw Man being created and the image of Man sitting at the Right Hand of the Power of God the Father. He knew that this creation would be above him and would rule over him for Eternity. So, in his defiance towards God, Satan would scheme a way to put a wedge between God and His Creation. He already knew from experience that disobedience is the highest order of rejection by God.

Now, the mystery in all of this is that the Lord God would allow Satan to oppose the Man and scheme a way to deceive him. Adam had no practical knowledge of 'Good and Evil'. He did not have the concept that these were forces opposed to each other, that one is the adversary of God, and the other is the very Nature of God. From the moment Adam became physically alive, he was spiritually conscience of the full identity and purpose of God as the Creator. Adam gazed upon the Presence of the Lord God and was in full communion with the Lord God, <u>one on one</u>. Even so, Adam was made from the dust (material) of the Earth and was not eternal in his physical attire.   What Adam reflected was the image of God in the Flesh…there was no other creature like Man in all of creation. He was created as body (physical), soul (mind or consciousness) and spirit (eternal image of God). His body (flesh) had an innate character of sin in it because it was made from the physical Earth. The flesh sin had not been activated in the man until he disobeyed the Command of God. When Adam obtained the knowledge of 'Good and Evil', the sin in his flesh became activated and his entire physical being became corrupted by that knowledge because he had put into action what he had learned. The Man had separated himself from the pureness of what God had purposed for him and enlightened in the knowledge and ways of sin. Thus, when the Man sinned against God, the Lord God decreed "*that the wages of sin is death*", and the Man began to die from that moment forward.

God retracted His authority from Man to rule in the Eternal (Spirit) on Earth. He had lost the power and authority of subduing the earth and all that was within it from the Eternal (Spirit) sense but not from the physical perspective. Man had given that authority and power over to the powers of darkness when Satan had cloaked himself in the shroud of an animal (a serpent) to deceive the woman (Eve), who in turn deceived the Man (Adam) by tempting him to disobey the Command of God. It was not until the Man had committed the act of disobedience that God passed His Judgment on Mankind as a sentence of blasphemy. His Judgment would include cursing the Earth as a resource against the Man, making toil a virtuous necessity in Man's daily existence for survival, until he would return back to the ground in which he came from. In the woman His Judgment would be a physical curse, increasing her trouble in pregnancy and increasing her pain in childbirth, yet in spite of this she would maintain a compelling desire for her husband (sexually and emotionally) and she would be subject to his authority and control (Master over her). Then the Lord God cast them out of the Garden, which He called Paradise, to the outskirts of the Earth where the natural forces of nature and the powers of darkness were waiting. From this venue Man began his struggle of life and the sentencing of death, which would follow all mankind because Man had become sin and imposed God's Judgment upon the physical creation…this would become the legacy of Man's disobedience and blasphemy. The Lord God would maintain His communion with Man through prayer and supplication but would no longer allow Man to look upon His Glory…God would mysteriously distance Himself.

When the Lord God set everything into existence, the auxiliary of Heaven was opened to creatures of worship and praise, and in the midst of the "Fire" of God was Himself, in the form of a Physical Being. This image was a mystery to all of the Hosts of Heaven until the Lord God revealed Himself on Earth as the man-child (Jesus the Messiah) in a stable in Bethlehem, Israel ~2000 years ago. Until Jesus the Messiah was born, all of the human creation was bound by God's Judgment against sin. Out of the Wilderness of Wondering, God brought forth a Nation of His own Chosen People (Israel) in which He would bring forth the supplications of the Law (*Torah*) and the warnings and directions of

31

the Prophets. The Torah (Law of Moses) was the standard by which God revealed His displeasure with Man's sinful condition and would be a constant reminder of the wedge that Man had made between spirit and flesh. The Prophets revealed action (present and future) that God would fulfill if Man remained in disobedience and blasphemy against the Will of God. The Law produced a Covenant between God and Man's sinful nature by imposing ritualistic events for man, to do in order to appease God's Wrath and Judgment. As the Jews continued to stagger from the path of Righteousness under the conditions of the Covenant established by the Law, the Lord God would reveal the purpose of His Will through the Prophets. As the Lord God established the nation of *Israel* under a Covenant by the Law, He was pronouncing His intention to all of the human creation for future reconciliation of their sinful condition.

Now, the mystery in all of this is that God would first reconcile a nation under a Covenant by the Law, and that this Covenant would be the foundation for all of the human creation to follow, until which time God would complete His Reconciliation with Man, through the Law, by His own personal sanctification and Blood Sacrifice as the Atonement of all sin through His Only Begotten Son, Yeshua Adonai, and release Mankind from their bondage and captivity to sin and His Judgment against all flesh...thus the wages of sin (*death*) would be deposed and replaced by Salvation through Propitiation and the Clemency of God. In doing so, *Israel* would become personally connected to the Will of the Father (God Himself), and take on a personage with God, that set them apart from the rest of the human creation by being called the Children of Israel or the Children of God. This implied that God was their Father, and that the image of The Father would be pronounced in every edict of their society and religion and would make them unique amongst all mankind. Because of this, the restraints against the Children of Israel were severe.

The Law, in and of itself, imposed conditions which would require Israel to isolate themselves from the rest of the world. God had dictated a strict ritual purity in order to fulfill a physical sanctification and allow a chosen representative of the nation to stand in proxy for the whole nation before the Presence of God. This representative was the High Priest. He would be giving Offerings and Sacrifices unto the Lord God in accordance with the prescribed methods outlined by God through the Law of Moses. All of the Imagery, Symbolism and Ritual of the High Priest pointed to the future representative (Jesus the Messiah), who would stand in proxy for all mankind before the Presence of the Almighty God, to be the High Priest of the Temple of God in Heaven and the Eternal Sin Offering, which would appease God's Wrath and Judgment forever. Yeshua Adonai proclaimed that, "*those who believe in Me shall never die but have Eternal Life* ", and He further proclaimed, "*I AM the Way, the Truth, and the Life, No one goes to The FATHER except through Me*".

Now, the mystery in all of this is that four thousand years prior to the coming of Yeshua, since the day Man was cast out of the Garden where God's physical Presence was, Adam and his seed (offspring –

Mankind) were under the Sentencing of Death because of sin.

Two thousand years prior to the coming of Yeshua, since the day that Abraham (*Avraham*) left his father's house in Ur, God created the nation of His people and proclaimed to them a Promise and gave the vision of a Promised Land, which would bring forth the birth and offspring of His Salvation for Mankind.

One thousand eight hundred years prior to the coming of Yeshua, since the day Jacob (*Ya'akov* - grandson of Abraham) would receive from God the transformation of his name to *Israel (Yisrael)* meaning '*God Struggles*', which identified him to the Everlasting Covenant that God promised to Abraham for the nation and produced twelve sons who would become the ancestors of the twelve tribes of Israel. That from Judah (*Y'hudah*) in Bethlehem (*Beit-Lechem*), God would establish the lineage to the Messiah (Yeshua *the Saviour*).

One thousand two hundred and fifty years prior to the coming of Yeshua, since the day Moses (*Moshe*) led the nation of His people out of Egypt in the Exodus, God transformed the nation, into representatives on Earth who would receive from Heaven what God had perfected in His Righteousness for sinful Man to live by...which was the Law (*Torah*). That God would establish His Tabernacle (*Dwelling House*) in the midst of the nation of His people, to perfect their worship and obedience under the first Covenant ordained by the Law.

One thousand years prior to the coming of Yeshua, since the day God proclaimed Saul (*Sha'ul*) as the first

King of Israel and established the nation of His people as a kingdom on Earth...that God would proclaim and anoint a new King (*David*), out of a sheep pasture as a young boy from Judah in Bethlehem (*Beit-Lechem*),
and that he would be the heir to the House of Israel and the lineage to the seed of Mashiach. That from the House of David would come the next King and heir (*Solomon- Shlomo*) to build the Holy Temple (*House of God*) and proclaimed that God had established permanence on Earth with the nation of His people, in the city of Jerusalem (*Yerushalayim*). That this place would forever be called the Holy City of God and be the place where God would proclaim His Salvation and sanctify all of the world.

One year prior to the coming of Yeshua, the prophecies that had foretold His birth and the setting of events that would verify His arrival as the Messiah were being fulfilled. A virgin chosen by God and the man whom she was to marry, who was from the House of David born in Bethlehem (*Beit-Lechem*), were to be the earthly parents of the Son of God. As God the Father, bestowed His Spirit, the woman conceived in Holiness a child that would have no sin...neither in body (*flesh*) nor soul (*mind*).   That through her husband, the child would have the human lineage of the House of David bestowed to Him as well...thus fulfilling the prophecy that the Messiah would be born of a virgin to the House of David.

Now, the mystery in all of this is that the coming of Yeshua marked the beginning of the fulfillment to God's promise for all Mankind...that their sins would be forgiven as well as forgotten...that the sting of death would no longer be a bondage to life, and that the Heart of God was going to be demonstrated to ALL of Mankind as Mercy. The nature of God is Love. The Lord said of Himself that" God *is Love*". Yeshua the Messiah sealed the New Covenant of God with His Love, "*for God so loved the world, that He gave His Only Begotten Son, so that everyone who believes in Him shall not perish but have Everlasting Life*". What God gave became the Sacrifice of His Body and Blood..."*the Blood of the New Covenant*", and with a new commandment, He set forth the order of what He called His Church..."*that you love one another as I have loved you*" and "*too love your neighbour as you love yourself, for in this resides the entire Law*".

To all my dear Brethren and those who are unsaved, through Yeshua HaMashiach, God was no longer demanding that Man carry out the act of a ritual, by making a sacrifice under the Law in order to redeem a nation for a period of time; but rather, He was now offering Himself as the Sacrifice which released All Mankind from the burden of their sin, which demanded the Law to be imposed. Therefore, we are no longer under the Law but through the Blood of the New Covenant of Yeshua (Second Part of the Godhead-the Man God), we have been rescued from the Wrath and Judgment of God and the Second Death. The First Death is the result of God's judgment against sin being engulfed in the body (flesh) of every human being. God has pronounced death as the result of sin in both the body and human spirit...the body goes to the grave and returns to the natural elements of the Earth, while the Eternal Spirit of the person waits in the darkness of the grave for the Day of Judgment. The Second Death is God's Judgment against the spirit of each, and every human ever born into existence who opposed the New Covenant (*this is called the Great White Throne Judgment*). It must be made very clear that in the Eyes of God, existence (*Life*) begins at the moment of conception in the womb. As the Lord God has mentioned in the Written Testimony (*the Bible*) and the Testimony of His Prophets, "*I knew you in the womb*" and "*from your seed shall I multiply a nation which cannot be counted in number amongst the stars*". It is evident that at the moment a man impregnates a woman with his seed, that through this act, God has commanded Life to begin and holds it accountable unto Himself. Nevertheless, every human being conceived is done into the innate character of Man's sin and will possess the sin nature from conception.

The outcome of God's Judgment of a person's Eternal Spirit into Damnation is the Second Death, for all who are found guilty of disobedience, blasphemy and rejection towards God's New Covenant through Yeshua HaMashiach, and whose names are not found in the Book of the Living, shall be cast into the Lake of Fire…which is the Second Death!

The Lake of Fire is an Eternal place where the Lord God will impose His Eternal Judgment and incarcerate sin forever. This is the Justice of God and is not negotiable between Himself and His Creation. It was intended for Satan and his fallen angels; but will be the destination of every human being whose heartfelt opposition and disobedience was against the Word of God and His Salvation (Yeshua the Messiah). The

Lake of Fire is a place of Eternal Separation and Torment, where the person feels the pain and burning associated with fire, where gnashing of teeth and screaming is prevalent, and utter agony prevails, yet the Fire does not consume the person ...as the Lord God has stated, "*anyone whose name was not found in the Book of the Living, was thrown into the Lake of Fire, and the smoke of their torment shall go up forever and ever without end*".

Now, the mystery in all of this is that the Lake of Fire exists in a chasm, separated far below the New Heavens and the New Earth (Book of Revelation, Chapter 21). It is like an ocean with no end to its horizon. Churning molten action, which gives the appearance of flames. The substance of the Fire is actually spiritual, and not substance of matter and energy as we know it in the physical universe. The Fire is the Love of God in its purity of Substance and Spirit. As the Lord says, "*My Love is as a burning fire which consumes all that stands before it*". In this the Lord is identifying His Being as all-consuming to the Creation, and He has complete Power and Authority over everything which stands before Him. God has created everything from Himself, the Nature and Presence of God is in everything, therefore, everything has the Nature of God in it. This means that God's Love is prevalent in everything He has created, in Heaven and on Earth (*the Physical Universe*). When the Lord God calls up the Creation to Final Judgment and separates the wheat from the chaff, He will be separating Himself from the Chaff (*sin*) and those who will be identified as sin. At the moment He passes Final Judgment and

38

Commands the unrighteous to be cast into the Lake of Fire, a metamorphous is completed in the spirit of these people. The innate Love of God is removed from their being forever and they become complete and total sin. They share the same outcome as Satan and the demonic beings who rejected the Love of God and were sentenced to Eternal Damnation. At this point God must turn His face away from them and their punishment, for the Lord has said, "*I cannot gaze upon their sin, nor will they stand in my Presence...I have forsaken the evil thing and have no communion with them*". In being totally opposite of the Nature and Will of God, these people and creatures now are tormented when thrown into the Lake of Fire, which is the purity and substance of the Love of God. It burns them in torment as the Love of God rejects the sin, which is incarcerated (*incarnate*) into their very beings forever.

My Dear Brethren, there is nothing which has been written in this letter that is untrue or false. The Holy Spirit of God has inspired and enlightened every word of it. As I send it out to the Church (*Body of Messiah*) throughout the world, I am reminded by the Lord God, that there is very little time left before the things which have been written and talked about regarding the End Times of the Last Days all come to pass. God's Love and Mercy surpass all understanding and is still going forth for ALL mankind to receive through (Yeshua the Messiah); but His Judgment is coming soon, and it will be swift and complete, and everlasting. The time is near for the return of Yeshua...for His Second Coming (*the Rapture*), which is for the Church..."*for the Lord Himself shall descend out of Heaven and in a shout*

39

(Command), with the Trump of God and the voice of the Archangel; and the dead in Messiah shall rise to life first and ascend unto the Lord in the Clouds; then we who are alive at that moment shall be changed, from mortal into immortal, and shall meet them in the air, into the cloud, and we shall always and forever be with the Lord". Then what will follow will be the Greatest Tribulation against Man and this world, the likes of which has never been seen before, since the beginning of all Creation. God's Wrath shall fall on this world and unto ALL mankind. for seven (7) years. He will break the Seals, sound the Trumpets, and pour out the Bowls of His Wrath on the Earth and make All of Mankind weep in bitter anguish. As for those who were part of the Body of Messiah, we are in the Presence of the Lord God in Heaven, partaking in the Marriage Feast of the Lamb. After the Lord calls the Church (*Past and Present*) unto Himself, we are being prepared to be presented by the Son (Yeshua Adonai) to the Father (ABBA YAHWEH) as His Bride…the Church becomes the Bride of Messiah and is presented as a gift to the Father forever. We sit at the Right Side of Messiah, and He sits at the Right Hand of the Power of God, the Father (ABBA YAHWEH).

Now, the mystery in all of this is that before the Lord God can end the physical Dispensation of Time and allow the preponderance of His own Nature and Will towards only 'Good' to triumph over the powers of darkness and the knowledge and value of Evil; He must allow Evil to accentuate beyond the purpose He had intended it for.

When the final battle against good and evil is fought, it is fought both in the heavenly realm (spirit) and the physical (flesh). It begins with Man against Man, but in the end, Satan once again tries to win and triumph over God by putting forth a last strong attempt to fight it out with the Heavenly Hosts. In his deception, he rallies all of the demonic forces against Man and against the spirits in the atmosphere of Earth. In his final attempt, he curses and blasphemes the name of the Lord God and all the Heavenly Hosts in the highest order possible…then claims to be God in the physical and sits in the Holy Place of the new Temple in Jerusalem as the Messiah incarnate; this is known as the "*Abomination of Desolation*". He makes all of mankind worship him as their god by having a mandatory requirement that no one can buy or sell any product or conduct any business or work unless they have his mark (*the mark of his name*) placed on either their forehead or right hand…this will be known as "*the Mark of the Beast*". In preparation for this, God has brought a great deception upon both spirit and flesh to where they both act in one accord. The Lord said that "*in the Last Days, the Father will send a spirit of deception to all Mankind…and if He did not shorten those days, even the elite* (Body of Messiah) *would falter and fall under its control*". This will be a spiritual wave of demonic force that has been held back since the foundations of the world were created, that God the Father will command to be let loose…this sets the premise for the Anti-Christ to subdue the earth and all mankind with the power of this great deception, to take the *Mark of the Beast* and believe that he is God.

41

The horror that will be revealed on the Great and Terrible Day of the Lord, is when Jesus the Messiah is sitting on the Judgment Seat of God and commands the Angel of the Lord to throw these people into the Lake of Fire. The Lord God, in His Divine and Holy Nature, is not only Love...but Justice as well. The Mercy of God towards the righteous demand's fulfillment of His Justice. In order for the fulfillment of ALL things to pass from sin into righteousness, under the allotted Dispensation of Time that God the Father has given within this physical realm, He must pass Judgment on all unrighteousness and cast it into the Lake of Fire, where it will be completely separated from His Presence forever. After this is completed, then the Lord God will resend His command of the Physical Creation, which has been going forth since the beginning of all creation, and all of the universe (physical heavens and Earth), will burn up and melt from intense heat, and with great noise, and be completely destroyed. The Lord God will put forth an Everlasting Command for a New Heavens and New Earth to be created, and from the Abode of God in Heaven, the Lord will restore the City of Jerusalem on the New Earth. It will be the City of God where Man will dwell forever and ever...*Amen.*

My Dear Brethren, in your reading of this, I charge you in the Name of the Most High God, Yeshua HaMashiach, to heed what has been written in this letter, for the Lord Himself has given utterance of these words and has directed me through His Spirit to write them down and send it to ALL of the Body of Messiah (*the Church*) throughout the entire world.

4

Message to the World
(Written in November 2018)

From Ken, who is a Believer in **Yeshua** ADONAI (**Jesus** the Lord), one who has received the Calling of God to be a teacher, and a witness to His Majesty and Holiness.

As I was worshiping and contemplating God and His Greatness, The Spirit of All Life opened before me a witness that I was encouraged to share with you all, for not everyone who reads this will share in His Testimony nor in His Presence without condemnation of the Eternal Judgment.

This is now the testimony of what God is giving through His loving but imperfect servant, in order that what He has shown may be made a credible witness to His Majesty and Holiness.

ADONAI was standing at the Fire Alter with His Arms extended, His Eyes like Brilliant Blue Sapphires, He was adorned in glistening brilliance, like shining diamonds brighter than the sun and He had a Golden Crown on His Head. His Face was so brilliant and radiant that all I could see was Pure Transparent Light coming from Him, not like the light from a lamp, but Pure Transparent Glory going in all directions forever; but behind the transparency I could see what looked like the image of a man's face but not in any detail, just that it was a man's face behind His Glory. When He spoke, all of Heaven quaked and everything fell in Worship towards Him. He was Commanding when the

Spirit spoke to me saying: "*God's Grace and Mercy is against us (It Opposes Us), because of the constant Sin Nature of our flesh (Human Nature); but because He has Complete Power and Authority over all aspects of the Creation and by His overwhelming display of Unconditional and Unwavering Love, He has chosen to forgive us all by Virtue of His Sustaining Love and our heartfelt willingness to exercise Faith in receiving the Word of God (Yeshua ADONAI) as the only recourse to Everlasting Life*".

His Power currently Sits with Him on the Throne of Mercy (The Mercy Seat) regarding things in Heaven and on Earth; but the Day is coming and is already here when He will then Sit on the Judgement Seat of God and Judge all of the Living and the Dead. No one will escape His Judgement, and it shall be the Righteousness of His Mercy and Grace that casts all who are not found in the Lamb's Book of the Living into the Eternal Fire and separation of His Damnation.

The Day is coming and is already here when Adonai shall gather His People (the Living and the Dead) together to the Assembly of the Most High, and the Radiance of His Glory. His Face is that of a billion suns shining through all of Eternity with Glory exceeding all that exists, above all things and high above the Heavenly Hosts, not even the Holy Beings that surround His Throne can gaze upon Him. His Kingdom is His Abode, and we shall have our rightful place sharing in it.

He is not a man, and we are not men in the form of our previous physical existence; but rather Spirit that is of

Everlasting Form and Glorified Substance just as He is. We are not like the Angels, but rather His Highest Order of Creation and the Heirs to His Salvation. We shall gaze upon His Glory and be given the Judgement of the Angels.

My Faithful Ones...be in One Accord with the Word of God (ADONAI) and not restricted by the Law or your guilt toward sin, but rather receive All Things in Righteousness, for He has allowed us to receive His Grace and Mercy and All Things in Righteousness through our Faith that has transformed us from being His Enemy to the Children of the Most High, and with that comes our inheritance.

Don't let the Enemy still your Inheritance by giving you a false hope or a false testimony that steals the Free Gift ADONAI has put before each and every one of us. This life is not the Free Gift from God, nor any form of abundance in this life. The birth that we have received through the flesh is not the Free Gift. The Free Gift from God is our release from the bondage of Death, Death which has come about because our inherent sin (disobedience and blasphemy) towards God, the Creator. Nothing in creation could redeem us from such a grievous disparity against the Holy God. He is Righteous in condemning us since mankind chose to rebel and stand in condemnation against the Holiness of God (the Creator).

Only God within Himself could render propitiation of our sinful character and the artifacts of sin which had accumulated before Him. His Purpose was to show His Power of Redemption through His Love in the form of

Grace and Mercy. Because Sin brought about the Law and it was the Law that was condemning us, then God had to fulfil all Righteousness through the Law Himself, thus nullifying the Atonement (Covering Over) of sin and bring about the absolute Forgiveness (Propitiation) of sin forever.

It is not the Spirit that needs to be redeemed, but the physical creation. Even though the Human Spirit is in need of being reborn, the Redeemer had to come as part of the physical human creation in order to do that. When Yahweh purposed Himself (Elohim) to redeem mankind, He did so as birthing the Man-God (HaMashiach Yeshua), the Second Part of the Godhead (Elohim) who was ADONAI. When Yahweh purposed Mashiach to redeem mankind unto Himself, he did so according to the Law under the Mitzvah of Atonement. This meant that in order for the Atonement to become Propitiation of sin, then Yeshua HaMashiach would stand in for the Blood Sacrifice and take the place of the Lamb to appease God's anger against all Sin and thus Render Eternal Forgiveness of Sin once and for all. By doing it this way, Yahweh was taking the symbol of the High Priest, the Temple and the Law of Atonement unto Himself (HaMashiach Yeshua) for all mankind Forever. There would be no need to continue the act any longer nor the fulfilment of the Law, which had been completed by Yeshua ADONAI. God has given complete Clemency to all mankind (Past, Present and Future).

Now, the mystery in all of this is that Yahweh purposed mankind to be not only forgiven of their transgressions against Him (Holy God), but to be completely redeemed so that humankind could stand before Him as a New Creature and share in His Kingdom. Therefore, Yeshua ADONAI would be the Eternal Sacrifice by His Death, but the act of redemption would have to extend to His Resurrection from Death to Life by the Power of Yahweh. Once this had been accomplished according to the Will of God, then the Power of Man's Redemption was through Yeshua ADONAI.

By honoring God's Eternal Sacrifice through your Heartfelt Faith that Yeshua ADONAI is Lord of your life and you need Him to be that Redemption, because you cannot save yourself by any means in this physical creation or of the world, then by calling upon His Name (Yeshua) and claiming him ADONAI (Lord) and confessing this as a proclamation with your mouth to others, then you shall be Saved. The Mystery and Miracle is that at that moment you do that and receive your salvation, your Dead Human Spirit is replaced within you by the Holy Spirit (Ruach HaKodesh). This also means that you have been purchased at a price by Yeshua, that you were a slave to Sin and are now a free man to His Salvation forever. So, the real Gospel is that *"Our Captivity to Sin is Over!"*

ADONAI calls all humans to be the Heirs of His Salvation, but for whatever reason, not all will heed the Call, and the Enemy steals their Salvation through deceptive measures, with desires of the sinful flesh and false testimony blaspheming the Word of God and turning many from the Truth. God does not call the righteous to repent and receive His Free Gift, but rather He is calling the sinner and unrighteous to repent and receive this Free Gift; but it takes courage and a determination to Love Him above all things and to believe that He is the Lord and God Almighty (*El Shaddai*).

The benefits to Receiving Yeshua into your heart and Faith are everlasting and beyond anything this life or this world could ever supply; and the rejection of Yeshua from your heart is beyond anything you could ever imagine in the horror of this life or this world, both are everlasting and Eternal...Time Without End! Only a Fool would reject the Salvation of God and Eternal Life in His Presence Forever, and only a Fool would embrace the desires of this world and this life which is temporal and receive the Damnation and Separation from God Forever.

Someone reading this needs to make a decision, Right Now!

5

What's the Link between Man and God?
(Written in January 2020)

What have we all done, that is so horribly wrong? What is this Curse that falls on all of us? Why is the constant call by Preachers and so called "Men of God" to Repent and call out to God for His forgiveness. As if every single thing that we have done all of our lives is but filthy rags. Holding this unseen Force called God over our heads claiming retribution if we don't succumb to His Will. Aren't they also sinners, preaching to you and me about stopping something that they themselves are guilty of? Or are they in a Special Class, exempt from the condemnation so they can freely accuse others without any retribution. How did they get the apparent stench of Sin off them?

Claiming that every act from the human heart is corrupted by Sin. What Sin? Where did it come from? How are we all infected with it? What is the definition of Sin and by who's definition is it, God, or Man's? I mean it is so ridiculous that everything can be called a Sin, it all depends on who you talk to or what group you associate with. According to some religions dancing is a sin, playing cards is a sin, having a glass of wine or beer is a sin, having sex is a sin; even when all of these things are called out in the Bible as righteous things to do.

I mean I don't deliberately go out of my way to do bad things or think about it. They call us Sinners and completely separated from God because of this condition. What does "God" have to do with anything? Who cares! I mean I didn't ask to be born, and then to have this mystique of being inherently evil with a sin nature born into us is too much to believe.

From birth you learn that there is Good and Bad, things that happen in this life can go in either direction. Then you learn about death and that it is an inevitable outcome that will happen without notice to every living creature on this planet, a crapshoot, rolling the dice and coming up with Snake-Eyes eventually. Then your told that Death is the outcome of Sin and God's punishment against it. Even though everything dies, we (Humans) are the only creatures that need forgiveness from God, not the animals, fish, birds, insects, only mankind. The Law seems to be for man only. The other creatures on this planet don't obey any of its statutes, they do whatever comes natural to them, instinctively. They hunt each other down, kill and feed off each other, there are no morals established for them like there are for humans. So, Sin seems to be an interaction between God and Us, something that has cause us to be a reprobate in His sight and made Him Pass Judgement on us, and we are born with this stigma from conception through birth. Even if you don't believe there's a God, it still exists and the apparent outcome of it is still the same.

Yes, there are acts being perpetrated out there by bad people, doing unspeakably disgusting things, but at the same time there are more acts of righteousness and good being done which overshadow the evil and becomes the standard of what Life, Liberty and the pursuit of Happiness is. It seems that Happiness and

Life in that perspective is what everyone is striving for, it's the universal norm; and that Evil is just something you must contend with and fight to overcome it, it is the adversary of the norm. So, until it attacks you, it is off in the distance and safely watched on the nightly news and heard about only by Hearsay, it's just the way life is, and you work around it and hope to avoid it. In this world you have Good and Evil. I didn't make the rules, this is what we are born into, and it's always been this way since the beginning of time. It appears that the majority of our Laws and these Rules that have been establish are from thousands of years ago and the origin is from the Bible, in particular, the Ten Commandments given to Moses. That they are edicts (also known as the Golden Rules) that have been establish for man by God and is the way He prefers that we uphold them, and if we do so, then all will go well for us; it is that established Universal Norm, it is the essence of what "Good" is.

From anyone's perspective, there are only two kinds of people, those that do "Good" and those that do "Bad". The 'Good Doers" chose to obey the Rules, the Law; and live a happy prosperous life under those constraints. The "Bad Doers" chose to disobey the Rules, the Law; and find themselves constantly interacting with Law Enforcement and being incarcerated or imprisoned, not living such a prosperous life outside of those constraints.

Who chose the Rules and Laws under those constraints and what set the precedence of the conditions? The evolution of man's social dignity comes by order of "Live and let Live". That you make Rules and Laws that allow each one of us to live in a society setting where people harbor Good-Will and Peace towards each other and anything adverse to that is punished or branded out by virtue of the Law.

But there seems to be another aspect with being a "Bad Doer", a sinister side called Evil. Something that compels them to do these acts against the norms of Rules and Laws, possibly for their own personal gratification or pleasure, or is there something else leading them on?

It's by choice that we make these decisions because each one of us is born exactly the same way, as individuals free to interact in our environment. Our individual circumstances of learning, making choices and lifestyles on how we live may be under an oppressive or non-oppressive manner, but nevertheless, we all come into this world free to interact with our environment.

What is the inspiration to do something that goes against the norm? To have a negative outcome to the situation you are creating, even if it means incarceration or loss of life, maybe your own. Some of this is a result of our anatomic being which is under the influence of a disease or some kind of physical affliction which brings about a mental illness, stress or self-induced trauma. Whatever the reason for such characteristics of negative "Bad" behaviour to manifest itself it can happen to any of us at any time throughout our lifespan. But, to become Sinister or Evil seems to imply an outside influence from a source which does not originate within our anatomic human being yet grossly influences it. It acts as if it is a separate life-force that commands and compels premeditated acts of violence and suffering, adversely against the Rules and Laws as if it is fighting it. Evil seems to want to inflict injury, mayhem, murder, chaos, utter destruction; it's not the same as just being "BAD", it's the extension of it through a non-human source, something else, but where does it come from and why do humans interact with it so complacently.

There seems to be a distinct difference between us (Humans) and all the rest of the creatures on this planet. It is indeed awestruck that out of all the approximately 8.3 million species on this planet (Approx. 2 million being animal types), that only Human Beings have the position among them as the Highest Order. We rule this planet completely, and in some manner, we manage or control everything within it, and act as if we have been given governance in that capacity instinctively. What is it that sets us apart from all the other species in existence?

On the Evolutionary Timetable we are known as Homo Sapiens, the last to just appear out of nowhere. Sapiens are a class of Vertebrate Mammals that stand upright and walk, endothermic (Warm Blooded) and have a highly developed brain, with a resultant capacity for articulate speech and abstract thinking (ultra-cognitive). Because we walk upright the angle and position of our brain stem going into the base of our brain, helps in giving us superior sensory and regulation of those functions. We have two Cerebral Hemispheres

(Lobes) to our brain like most other mammals with one big exception, we have a 6-layered neocortex network that connects both hemispheres allowing us higher brain order functions.

Putting aside our superior mental capabilities, there are a few other characteristics that uniquely set us apart from all the other species. One is our uncanny ability to reason and give intelligent thought and analysis to any situation, our inventive capability to industrialize and form advanced societies, grow and cultivate our own food, but most evidently another is, that most Human's identify to a Spiritual Awareness or connection to a Divine Presence, whether it is based upon a philosophy, metaphysical awareness, or a religious conviction, it is by definition called Faith. But, to define what Faith is, can only be explained as something unseen or intangible from our five senses, it's a belief. It could be described as a mental condition or philosophical reasoning which transcends our mortal being. It can be something you believe in and connect to that is higher in power or ability than yourself. It could be an extension of something greater than the physical environment or even considered Supernatural. Mostly, it is associated with a belief in a Higher Power or Guide that helps us down a pathway through life, or it can be equated to God as a Divine and All-Powerful Being, a Protector and Over-Seer. Then there's those people who choose to have Faith in themselves for self-perseverance and the personal strength to endure and overcome Trials and Tribulation. And of course, there's always others who claim that they have Faith in

Nothing, which is impossible, because of how the human psyche is conditioned to learn and transfer subconscious thoughts through sensory expression, your mind ends up conditioning you to believe in something by proxy; the denial is usually their arrogance to rebel against the thought of believing that there is something above them.

If you are honest with yourself, it's impossible not to wonder about God and Him having a part in all of this as being a Creation, rather than an uncontrolled circumstance were cosmic materials and amino acids congealed over millions of years which mysteriously evolved into perfect order. And we as the highest order of that evolutionary process supposedly came out of all of this in some pathway from a slime into a fish or bird, then into primates and without any link, all of a suddenly we appear (Humans) on the earth, and master's over all the other species. It just doesn't add up, and the person that thought of it ended up denouncing his theory, saying he just couldn't justify a premise for it any longer. No one can find that connection which adds us (Homo Sapiens) to the Evolutionary Timetable; the infamous "Missing Link", because there isn't one, it's a hoax.

There appears to be premeditated architecture and design throughout the universe, and with us. Where the Laws of Physics and Mathematical Quantum Intercession applies across the entire universal spectrum. If there are some inconsistencies, they're being allowed and are intertwined as part of the overall design, it helps to compliment and stabilize itself.

Science and the Bible agree on one thing, in the beginning all matter that we now see, the entire universe came out of nothing. A pinpoint of matter which exploded into everything we can see in the physical creation. It is totally inconceivable for science to equate, that from Nothingness came the entire content of the physical universe.

The acceptable theory and axiom are that there was a beginning pinpoint of condensed substance and energy the size of a trillionth of an atom of hydrogen, and that in an undetermined instant, it exploded outward 360 degrees with such extreme velocity and force, that within the first 3 seconds, 90% of all the known mass of the universe was expelled. As if it was a little hole coming forth through a tremendous veil, bursting forth the unmeasurable force of substance and heat (in the Trillions of degrees) that what was behind it. It wasn't until 380,000 years after the initial Explosive Event, or "Big Bang", that the universe had cooled enough for atoms to begin forming and Quantum Physics was being birth.

Something was behind that Veil of Nothingness which spewed forth all that we see before us. Could that something be GOD?

You first have to have the Faith in believing that there is a God who created everything that exists, and because He is the Creator of "All Things", including Human Beings, it's His decision to determine how it all interacts with Him and what the order is (Rules and Laws) so that Creation abides within His Will and His Purpose for it to exist. You also have to believe that the Bible is the only Written Testimony in which God is conveying His Purpose to mankind; all other sources are a counterfeit and even though they mention some truth in them, they mix in a lie through their doctrine which nullifies any Truth spoken by God. It is through His Spirit (the Holy Spirit) that He continues to reveal all Truth concerning Himself and the relationship He wishes to have with all people. He has given us a free will to accept or ignore those conditions (Statutes of the Law and Rules) thus placing ourselves "In His Favour" or "Against His Favour".

Why does this matter to any extent that we offend God?

We (Humans) have been created in the likeness of Him, through His Spirit. We are Spirit Beings having a Physical Human Experience. This is how we share in His likeness. It is His Spirit which is inside of each and every one of us (the Life Force) that reflects the likeness of God, who is Spirit. This is why God said, "You are gods" (Ref: Psalm 82:5-7, John 10:34), which refers back to the beginning of what God intended when he created Humankind, "Let Us make man in Our Image, after Our Likeness." (Genesis 1:26). He was speaking to Himself as the "Trinity". God is Three-Fold (Elohim) yet one God (ABBA-Father, Yeshua ADONAI-Son, Ruach HaKodesh-Holy Spirit). We as well are three-fold (Human) yet one person (Body-physical, Soul-mind, Spirit-Eternal Life Force-which comes from God). This is what ties us to Him in our order of Creation and our standing with His Eternal Purpose to exist as the Highest Order of His physical Creation. This was God's Purpose and Will, that in His physical creation He Himself would have a Physical Representation of His Essence as a Physical Being and that Being would be the highest order of His Creation (Human-Man). That's why we all-of-a-sudden appeared on earth. He created the earth and all that was within it first (every creature on land, in the waters, and in the air, and every creeping thing), then Man was formed out of the earth (ground) molded and God breathed His Holy Spirit (Eternal Life-Force) into the Man, and he became a Living Being.

We Humans will always be an Eternal Being, it's what God has Purposed in His Creating us. His intent is to fellowship with us forever, but there is one loophole that has occurred, Sin! When the first man (Adam) was created, and the first woman (Eve), they blasphemed a Commandment that God had given to them; to not eat the fruit from the Tree of the Knowledge of Good and Evil or they would surely die. As the Bible reveals it to us, the woman Eve was deceived by a serpent (disguised as the Evil One – Satan) to partake in eating of the forbidden fruit, saying that if she did eat of it, she would not die, but instead have wisdom and be like God. Now, Eve had pondered this for some time, being tempted to reach out to the tree and its fruit which was so very beautiful and pleasing to her. So, in the cool of the evening while the Man slept, she reached out to the tree again, but this time the Tempter was waiting for her and was eagerly wanting to eat of its fruit that God had Commanded the Man not too. She did partake in eating of it and when she did, a veil was lifted from her eyes and from her mind, and instantly she had the

Knowledge and Wisdom of God in knowing what Good and Evil was and another thing occurred, she did not physically die. So, she immediately went back to the Man and gave him some of the fruit and told him what had happened, and he did eat of it, and he too had Wisdom and did not physically die.

Now God does not give Orders, like we do. When He speaks, He does so through Commandments. These are Holy and come from the Throne of God and are Eternal. They will not be retracted and hold whatever consequence He assigned to them. In the Eyes of God, breaking or disobeying a Commandment is Blasphemy and His Judgment must be served as a result. This was the point at which to Man committed Sin against a Holy God because of the Blasphemy he had committed. The communion between God and Man had ended and Man became of Reprobate in the sight of God, He could no longer look upon nor fellowship with the Man (or woman) in Holiness, but in the darkness of sin He must reject them. He retracted the Holy Spirit that he had given to the Man, and now the spirit that dwelt within him was a dead human spirit, destined for death and the grave (Sheol). This was the outcome of Man's disobedience and God's Judgement against sin.

God morphed them into physical sin and darkness fell upon them. With that the reproductive seed of Man and conception of the woman was also morphed, so that every human being born out of and conceived from that moment forward would be born into sin. When the Man sinned, the whole planet, and all the creatures started to die as well. When Man fell from Grace, it influenced everything.

Therefore, a barrier had been created between God and Mankind, and Man would have to repent for the sin he had become in the sight of God and everything that Man did throughout his whole life would be nothing but filthy rags in appeasing a Holy God's Wrath against their sin, generation after generation, after generation.

Adam had relinquished to Satan and the Powers of Darkness all of the inheritance he had received from God over the world and over all of the nations and governments that would come about. The power to rule was now his, and he was ready to receive it when Adam had surrendered to the woman and blasphemed against the Commandment of God.

The Bible says that God is Love, and He is Holy. So where is the Hope for Mankind in getting redemption for the sins that they perpetrated against this Loving and Holy God?

Believe it or not God had a Purpose behind Man's fall from Grace and bring it about that He could redeem all mankind and forgive them of every sin, casting it as far away from His memory as the East is from the West. And in doing so, secure a pathway for Salvation and Eternal Life for all who would receive it. The key here is for all who would receive it. Because of our inherent "Free Will" that God has given us, it's not something that He would forcefully make us do. It's up to each individual person to make that choice, and by Faith acknowledge that forgiveness of sin has been bestowed on us along with the Gift of Salvation and Eternal Life.

So, how did God do this miraculous work of redeeming mankind and why would He do it? He did it because from the beginning He wanted fellowship and worship from His Creation, that was the Purpose in the first place for Creation.

He used the Law to bring about the Forgiveness of Sins and Himself to fulfill it, as well as the redemption of our Salvation and the promise of Eternal Life. What God did to bring us back unto Himself and allow our fellowship once more, was pure Love out of Holiness.

Three Thousand-Three Hundred years ago, God Commanded the Law to Moses for the nation Israel and eventually to all of mankind as a source of restoration. Israel would be the representation for the whole of humanity in which His Forgiveness and Salvation would come through, so the Law was the established Order that mankind was given to follow, in order to appease God's Wrath of mankind in his fallen state of sin. It would not give man reconciliation with God but would keep God from having to rebuke and cast Man out of His Presence because of our continued blasphemy towards Him.

In the Law, God gave Man a way of Atoning for their sins. This was the Law of Atonement known as "Sabbath of Sabbaths", (Ref: Leviticus 16:29-34) or in modern times Yom Kippur and was required to be performed once a year. An atonement is a covering over of, in this case, the debt of sin. God was not clearing the debt against mankind but was just allowing it to be accumulated without passing judgement against them. The debt would finally have to be paid "In Full" at a later time and by a means that God could give final Propitiation for the entire debt of all our sins and give us all final Forgiveness without any conditions. This was done by sacrificing a symbol of what God Himself considered to be a humble and pure source. He chose a lamb, that had no spot or imperfection on it (Flawless), which would carry the entire burden of the people's sins on it, and would be a Blood Sacrifice and Burnt Offering, thus giving Atonement for the entire year. This is what was demand by God, a Blood Sacrifice, in order for Him to overlook the sins of the nation that were before him. If this was not allowed, then He would have to deal with it and them in Final Judgement.

Two-Thousand years ago, God put into action what He had been purposing as foretold by the Prophets Isaiah, Jeremiah, Micah, Hosea the Psalms and even Moses, concerning the Messiah (Man-God) coming to earth, to represent God as the Second Part of the Godhead, the Son of God. God is Elohim, (Three out of One). He is Triune yet still is the same One God (Father, Son and Holy Spirit). These are not separate individuals, but personages of the same Source, out of One Being or Spirit. It is very difficult for us as a physical creation, born from physical parents to not think of the Son of God as being a separate individual aside from the Almighty, but He is from the same Source (Elohim) as God, the representation of us in Physical form. All that was Created was Created by Him and from Him, not one thing that was created was Created without Him.

He was born of a virgin, for He was conceived by the

Holy Spirit, to be human like, so that we could relate to everything he said and did. It was, "God with us". He would fulfill the Law and become that Sacrificial Lamb of God appeasing His wrath against us, giving Propitiation of all sin (Debt Paid in Full), and would conquer death by being raised from the dead, thus giving all would Believe in His Name, their Salvation and gift to Eternal Life (Being written in the Lamb's Book of the Living), having a share in His Kingdom forever.

The Messiah would become the First Born out of God, replacing Adam as the First Born out of the earth, yet created in the Image of God. So, the First Born out of God had to become a man in order to represent mankind. Yeshua bar Yosef, as He was known, or Jesus of Nazareth, was and is the Son of God. He was and is the Messiah, and He would free us from our captivity in sin and death, by means of being that Atonement Lamb of God who would die for our sins and then three days later be raised from the dead thus conquering death and the grave. For everyone that would believe in His Name and would repent acknowledging in a heartfelt way that they have sinned against God, and proclaim Him as Lord and God, and follow Him, they shall be Saved from all sin and have their names written in the Book of Life and receive their Salvation and Eternal Life forever. They will end up standing before God fulfilling His purpose, just as Adam would have, had he not fallen into sin. They will be blameless and called the sons and daughters of the Most High.

Now it should be told that this is the outcome for all who believe that God's Propitiation of Sin and Salvation is through Yeshua ADONAI (Jesus the Christ), but there is still the Judgment and outcome for those who refuse the Son of God and His Salvation. Theirs is the fate of an enemy of God and the Judgement he has pronounced against sin as being death and the grave (Sheol), but on the Day of Final Judgment, when the living and the dead are raised up, he will cast all those whose names are not found in the Lamb's Book of the Living (The Book of Life) into the Lake of Fire (this is the Second Death), where the Devil-Satan and the Powers of Darkness had already been thrown, and there they will be separated from God in torment forever. This is not something He chooses to do, it will be a sad day for the Son of God, tears will be streaming from His eyes as He must pass the Judgment on them; His Creation, that which He made to fellowship with Him and Loves; but because He is Holy and cannot look upon their sin which they have chosen to be, He separates them and the punishment for blasphemy is Eternal Damnation.

If you are reading this, then you are still alive and can make that choice, but because you have read this and heard the Truth, it stands as a witness against you.

Make your decision wisely, for no one knows when or for "Whom the Bell Tolls… it Tolls for Thee!".

6

Why Must We Reconcile to God?
(Written in September 2020)

To every Liar who gives false testimony to the Truth, I can without doubt tell you that you will give an account very shortly to the One Who Is and Who Was, and Who Is to Come Again. You Shall be on your knees, confessing that He is Lord and God! And your confession will not save you at that time, in fact it will condemn you, for you will have fallen into Utter Darkness and Eternal Damnation!

To all who know the Truth and proclaim His Name to the Glory of God the Father, I can without any doubt, assure you that you Shall pass from the darkness of this life, into the Glorious Light of His Eternal Presence. That God Shall lift you up and give you His Eternal Life, which Lives Forever (Time Without End).

But, for those who are Liars and who defame the Name, which is Above All Names (Yeshua ADONAI – Jesus the Christ), yours will be an Eternity outside of His Glorious Presence, you will be cast into Utter Darkness, with the Powers of Darkness waiting the Final Day of Judgement. Yours will be one of Eternal Death and Separation from Life, cast into the Lake of Fire Forever (Time Without End).

For God has appointed a Day when All Things Shall End, and All Things are made New Again. That the Old Things have passed away, and He Makes All Things New Again. This occurs first, when the curse of Adam is manifested and the Spirit of Death calls you out of this world and you are either cast into Utter Darkness (Sheol), completely separated from Life; or you are drawn towards the Glorious Light of His presence, awaiting the moment when the Spirit of Life within you is joined with what God has made to live in His Presence Forever.

For until the time which God has appointed, and the end of all things of this wicked age finally occurs, death has a purpose in fulfilling God's Will for each and every one of us. Yet in these Last Days of the End-Times, not all shall die, but some shall be withdrawn in a moment, in the twinkling of an eye, in order to fulfil what God has prophesied; *"Behold, I show you a mystery; for ADONAI (the Lord) Himself will descend from heaven with a shout, with the voice of the archangel, and with the trumpet of God. And the dead in Yeshua (Jesus) shall rise first, then we who are alive (in Yeshua) shall be changed, from mortal to immortal, and meet them in the air and so shall we be always with ADONAI (the Lord)"*.

So many of you believe that death is just part of life, part of the cycle of life. This is another lie that liars believe and profess. Death is a Curse; it is the outcome to the punishment of sin. It occurs in each of us because sin is encased throughout each of us, it is the fiber of our human being from conception through birth. Therefore, the proclamation from the Creator (God) to the first Man and beyond, was that because you have sinned a Curse is placed on us all, you shall beget Death!

The Life Force inside each of us is not a replication of human interaction, but the Command of God to the first man, he had created to be fruitful and multiply. That he (Adam) would reproduce in the same manner that God had created him and that was through Spirit into physical manifestation, for God is Spirit. God had created a human being physically (an empty shell) from the substance of the earth, then breathed into him His Spirit of Life, and man became a Living Being and thus created in the Image of God (Elohim-Eternal Spirit). This is the uniqueness of the Human Being, that we are Spirit Beings having a Human Experience. Out of all the physical creation on earth, God has only instilled His Spirit (Kodesh) into His Human Creation. All of the other living creatures He has created have life in them, but not His Spirit of Eternal Being.

Therefore, a person's Spirit is Eternal in the Image of what God has Created to be standing before Him in Eternity, and the flesh (physical body) covers and carries that which is Eternal through this physical universe here on earth; and when because of sin, the flesh dies, the Human Spirit must depart from the body and follow the pathway in which the person has prepared for it.

There is a condition that determines where the Human Spirit translates too. All human beings are pre-conditioned to fall under the Curse of Death at the moment of conception and beyond due to the inherent sin and morphed spiritual condition which has been transferred from the first human (Adam) to all of his offspring (Human Race); the "*Sin Gene*". In the Eyes of God, in His Presence, this is an evil state of existence and brings us under the Judgement of God and separates us from any communion with Him.

Therefore, the Righteousness of God and His Holiness proclaims that, "*No one is righteous, not one, for all have sinned and fall short of the Glory of God.*" God in all of His Righteousness has proclaimed that man was created perfect with all of the ability to stand before His Holiness and was intended to live forever in His Presence, but that Man chose willfully to disregard the Command of His Holy Order and instead, followed the path of temptation outside the Will of God's Holy Purpose and Blasphemed the Will of God. This now was an unreconcilable act and condition God called "Sin" and pronounced Judgement against it as Death. That immediately Adam was removed from his Eternal Life standing in the Presence of God (Spirit first, then flesh), into one that was cast out of His Presence through Death and eventually to the Grave (Sheol).

Time and Passing (Aging) is the outcome to the fallen state of God's Judgement against sin, and that eventually the flesh would succumb to Death through it. God created Human Beings in a three-fold manner as: Body, Soul and Spirit. The Spirit is the portion of our Being that is tied directly to an Eternal Destination outside of the Physical Creation. Once the body suffers the Curse of Death, our Spirit is forced out, either to be cast away to the Grave and the Tormenting Darkness waiting until the Final Day of God's Judgement, or be ushered into the Dazzling Presence of God, awaiting the moment when God will unite an Eternal Being (Body) with the Spirit of the person standing before Him. At that moment, we will become Spirit Beings having an Eternal Experience.

Truth prevails over a lie!

God said, "*I AM the Truth, The Way and The Life, no one goes to the Father except through Me*." It must be totally recognized and understood, that Jesus (*Yeshua*) the Christ (*HaMashiach) is both Lord (Adonai) and the Triune God (HaElohim).* The First-Born Son of Creation; Who Is, Who Was and Who Is to Come Again; The Alpha and The Omega, The Beginning and The End; The One who sits at the Right Hand of the Power of God; who is the Almighty and Eternal God.

By the Proclamation of His Word, The Son of God (Yeshua ADONAI) will reconcile all of mankind back to the Original Order of Creation, and through His Death and Resurrection from Death, has conquered Death and the World of the Dead (Sheol); and all who believe in Him shall receive the Gift of Eternal Life and have their names written in the Lamb's Book of the Living. Even though they may suffer physical death waiting for the Day of the Lord, they will be standing in the Presence of Almighty God waiting for the Glorious Day when God will make All Things New; and cast Death and the World of the Dead and everyone who was not found in the Lamb's Book of the Living into the Lake of Fire.

The Mercy and Love of God is speaking to someone right now, I hope you are listening and will receive the Free Gift of Eternal Life through Faith in Yeshua ADONAI (Romans 10:9-13); and free yourself from the Curse of Death and the Eternal Judgement that follows it. God has reconciled us back unto Himself through our heartfelt confession in Faith, Faith in the Son of God, Yeshua ADONAI (Jesus the Christ), who is the Living God. (1John 5:19-20)

In our mortal state of being, we humans can appease every condition and circumstance with justification and logical assumption that we are inherently "Good" and that evil is just a state of mind and superstition which can be overcome by good deeds and self-righteous attempts to "Do Better". If we faltered then the favorite saying for most people that don't want to admit that they are sinners is, "I'm only human" and this enfranchises their imperfect condition with nature and disregards any fallen state with God.

The unfortunate Truth, whether we admit it or not, is that we are created by God as Eternal Beings who have been created for His Pleasure and Purpose; and according to the Creator, we are in a State of Fallen Reconciliation with Him. It is imperative that we be reconciled back to Him in Righteous Standing because we will someday die in our human being and return to God through the Life-Force that we were originally created from (Spirit). Once this occurs, we needed to be prepared for the outcome of either standing before Him in Final Judgement to be Condemned or Glorified by Him. The Crossroad that we will be at is facing Eternity in one of two directions, either Separation (Damnation) from God or Life Eternal (In His Presence) with God.

Cry out to God...Confess yourself to God...Come to God-Yeshua ADONAI (Jesus the Christ) the One who is holding His Arms out to you, willing and waiting to receive you unto His Great and Mighty Presence. Humble yourself before the Almighty, your Protector and Saviour.

Be steadfast in Faith and know that **He is God**!

Yeshua ADONAI is Lord and God
(1John 5:20)

7

The Calamity of the "Last Days of the End-Times"
(Written in February 2022)

To the Believers of the Way, the ones whose names are written in the Lamb's Book of the Living; from your brother Ken, who is an Elder in the Church and who has been called by the Great God and Saviour Yeshua ADONAI, to be a Teacher and Witness of what is being spoken by the Spirit so that you will be aware of your place in all of this.

In Matthew, the 24th Chapter, Yeshua ADONAI (Jesus the Lord) prophesied regarding the Last Days of the End-Times and what the Signs that would be (Signs of the Times) of His Return and the End of the Age. His Disciples were very concerned about His departure from them, leaving then feeling insecure, so they were questioning Him about when He would be returning as He had promised, thinking that it would be within their lifetime.

The End Times have been recognized as being from the first generation of the Church, after Yeshua ascended from the Mount of Olives to this current generation (Moment in Time). This is known as "The Church Age" and will continue until the "Taking Away" (Rapture) of the Church out of this world. This of course will be a Supernatural occurrence, but nevertheless, one that God has promised He shall perform, and ADONAI keeps His Promises.

For 2000 Years, all the generations which have come

before us, have done so under the Hope that their generation would be the Last Generation before the Coming of ADONAI's return, but the Signs of the Times that Yeshua spoke of were not set in their full capacity yet.

It is in the Revelation of Yeshua ADONAI given to His Apostle John that we are given the mystery and the layout of the entire Church Age by referencing Seven (7) Churches in Asia Minor as to their temperament, loyalty, and faithfulness *(Revelation Chapters 2 and 3)*, this would set the stage for the entire Church Age. Each Church represents a distinct timeframe passing from one to the other that would make up the entire span of the "Time of the Gentiles". A timespan in which God would set aside dealing with Israel and would bring Salvation and the Good News (Gospel) to the heathen nations through what He referred to as His Church.

The emphasis on our current dispensation of time is with the Seventh Church known as Laodicea, meaning that we have already passed through six (6) Dispensations of the Church Age and are now in the Final One. Yeshua refers to it as the "Lukewarm Church", meaning it is neither Hot nor Cold, indecisive in their Faith and their Testimony of the Truth, willing to embrace tolerance and turning a lie into the truth and truth into a lie; so, because of this condition, He says that "I will vomit you out of my mouth". This is a profound statement for God to say, and the understanding of its meaning is even more unexplainable. What it means is that the Worldwide Church will become so cardinal and preaching tolerance for the world (a different Gospel) within the Body of Believers, that God will reject them to the extent of extreme measures and the Church shall fall under great persecutions and judgement. Even to the extent of causing the faithful to doubt and break away from the Truth, therefore the Father will shorten those days or else no one would survive, but for the sake of the elect (Faithful in Christ) those days (Final days of the End Times) will be shortened. We can all admit that never before in our lifetimes does it feel like time has sped up. Each day, each month, each year seems to go by more quickly unbeknownst to us, and when you realize it, it's like something supernatural is taking place.

The conditions of what are mentioned in the 24th Chapter of Matthew is what brings about the environment for Laodicea. It ushers in a "New World Order" of "Lawlessness" and "Godlessness", inherent with diversity, diverse religious ideologies, false religions and heresy, increase in the occult and political insurrection which infiltrates the Church. That there will be an increase in knowledge and technology, that there would be an increase in events with nature and the earth (Earthquakes with higher magnitudes, increased Volcanic Activity, Extreme Global Weather Events), that there will be wonders in the heavens and cosmic undertakings, that there will be a world-wide global spreading of hate and dissention, wars and continuous rumors of wars, that people everywhere will hate each other to an unprecedented level without self-control, where love grows cold, engaging in self-gratification and instead of lovers of God and seeking Faith, that all forms of abominations and perversion will be enacted and accepted and spread throughout the world, that a lie will become the truth, and the truth becomes a lie, that brother will turn against brother and murder will become common place and unpunishable.

The rise in Technology and Knowledge is an important revelation because it will be more than any other since the beginning of all human history until this moment in time; and that it would give rise to demonic manifestations such as described in Revelation Chapter 13. One such demonic manifestation of this technology is the use of Artificial Intelligence (AI), developed in the early 21st Century, and as demonstrated in the ability of the Anti-Christ to give life to an Image, called the "Image of the Beast", and make people succumb to its will. Another part of the prophecy is to have the ability to track every person on earth and label them with a Branding or Mark, called the "Mark of the Beast" also described in Revelation Chapter 13. This is where the Anti-Christ will impose his Mark, possibly to be laser etched or have an implant under the skin on either the right hand or forehead of every person on the planet. If you refuse to comply you will not be able to buy or sell anything, and you risk extermination by virtue of becoming an Enemy of the State. All of this is now possible through our technology with the internet cloud storing every bit of information on all of us, 5G internet speed and storage of personal data, thousands of terabytes worth daily; every person owning a handheld cell fone capable of capturing your whereabouts via GPS and every word you talk about. So never before in human history has this kind of technology existed or the fulfilment of this kind of prophecy been possible. But, along with this comes a Great Warning from God to not take the Mark of the Beast under any circumstance for there will be great punishment associated with worshiping the Beast and taking his Mark.

Another prophecy fulfilled in the Last Days of the End-Times is that Israel would reclaim their homeland and from the four corners of the earth, their people who had been scattered for 2000 years would return to the land of Israel and build a new homeland. This event occurred on May 14,1948 after Israel won their War of Independence from the Arab Nations and Palestine was once again in Zion control, and again in 1967 during the Six Day War when Israeli Forces captured and regained the West Bank of the Jordon River, the Golan Heights and the Old City of Jerusalem. From this Israel was recognized as a sovereign nation and Jews from all over the world started returning to the Homeland promised to them by God through Abraham. The significance of this event is that throughout history there has always been wars and rumor of wars, evil and mayhem spread throughout the world, earthquakes and upheavals in the earth, mysteries in the sky, all manner of mankind at their worst; but what would be the prophetic event that we should be looking to for all these things to be happening at the same time is with the restoration of Israel and the worldwide sojourn of Jews back to their ancestral homeland. This marks the generation that will not pass away before the Return of ADONAI, and it has been occurring in this current time and dispensation of the Church.

Yeshua spoke of the time when He would return for the Church and claimed that no one would know the day or the hour; not the Angels in Heaven, nor even the Son, but only the Father (YAHWEH) knows and has set the time for this event to happen. It is a mystery of the Father, and we should be prepared at any moment for it to happen.

It appears that although every prophecy mentioned about the Return of Yeshua has seemingly been fulfilled, we are still waiting on Father God to release us from this burden that binds us to this world. Even though we are not part of this world from a renewed sense, (Spirit in Body), this body still resides alive in this world, so it has influence on us. Once this captivity is release and our body dies or is instantly renewed through the event of the Rapture, our Spirit goes to ADONAI.

One thing to remember, is that everyone who is "Born Again", has been renewed as a New Creation with their New Names written in the Lamb's Book of the Living and has received into them the Holy Spirit which brings to Life our dead human spirit, and with Him comes the Mind of Yeshua ADONAI. He is the Revealer of the Truth and reveals everything to us about Yeshua. What the Spirit sees is revealed to the Church as a Witness of what Yeshua is conveying, for He is an extension of the same God. The Father, through Yeshua has sent the Holy Spirit as the "Helper" on our behalf in order to fulfill the promise when He said, "*I will never leave you or forsake you*", and "*I am with you always*".

It is the prerequisite for receiving your salvation, and forgiveness of all our sins and casting them from His Memory as far as the East is from the West.

The Calamity of the "Last Days of the End-Times" is that we are living in the most diverse, perverted, and evil times in our human history since the Days of Noah), and our outcome should be that of Sodom and Gomorrah. But YAHWEH has purposed this so that all righteousness could be fulfilled, and He may bring Judgement upon all of humanity for their continued wickedness and turning away from His Appeal for Righteous Standing in Yeshua ADONAI, whom He had sent to be the Saviour of all mankind and Propitiation of all sin forever, AMEN.

The Church must remember its First Love, for God Loved us First, then we Loved Him, and to tell of the "Good News" to all the world, **that our captivity to sin is over**. But to remember that by proclaiming this "Good News" (Gospel) you will suffer great hardship in these Last Days even unto death for your faith, but have courage in knowing that Yeshua ADONAI has overcome all things, and authority has been given to Him over all evil and the Powers of Darkness, thus by Faith, we too have that same power.

Fear is not from God, and He does not want us to be intimidated by anyone for preaching the "Good News" (Gospel). So therefore, my brethren, go forth in Power and Love knowing that this "Good News" has been ordained by God and not to fear any man and wear the protection of the Full Armor of God yet Fear God in

Righteousness and give your life to Him and for Him so that you may in righteousness, standing on the Day of Judgement before Him.

8

The Beast and the Dragon
(Written in May 2022)

From Ken, who is an Elder in the Church and by Faith proclaims this message to be one of truth and acknowledgement from the Spirit of ADONAI and is revealed as such for His Purpose.

There are prophecies and events mentioned in the Bible that are specific to the Last Days of "The End-Times". [The Book of the Prophet Daniel Ch 2, 7, 8 and 9; The Book of the Prophet Ezekiel Ch 38, 39 and 40; The Book of the Prophet Jeremiah Ch 12 verse 14, Ch 15, Ch 31 verses 8-10 and Ch 33 verse 7; The Book of the Prophet Isaiah Ch 12]. But more specific are the words spoken and prophesied by Yeshua ADONAI (Jesus the Lord) in the 24th Chapter of the Book of Matthew, and by the Revelation of Yeshua ADONAI given to the Apostle John in the Book of Revelation.

These have profound imageries that project a message that can only be interpreted through the Spirit of God. Even the one being given the prophecy didn't understand what it meant at the time, only the reader in the future time it was directed towards could understand its meaning due to the fact that those events being foretold were then and now unfolding and even the technology used to manifest the prophecy wasn't in place yet.

There are so much symbolism and paradoxical phrasing used in the Bible that it sometimes seems to be shrouded in mystery and mystical conjecture, and in retrospective observation as a reader, you often wonder how to find the meaning or purpose in the content. They are many times written to reflect the current historical moment in which these events were lived in. Others are a reflection of prophecy and have meaning to events and time in the future. In the case of prophecy, the symbolic images are used as a standard axiom for the current historical event and may be shared in the Signs of the Times for a future event (having no less than the same meaning, just a different point in history).

In many instances the imagery that is being described is in a form that is familiar to something in our physical creation here on earth and we recognize, but has a counterpart in Heaven, before the Presence and Abode of God, which is Holy and cannot be shared here on earth because of the sin that exists, so it is hidden from us and something that has never been seen or spoken of before in our physical creation. These come through Visions, Dreams and actual Visitations in which God reveals to whomever He chooses. Some have been revealed through the Prophets and the Apostles and recorded in the Bible, and some are still being revealed today and throughout Church History through The Spirit of God to people He has given Revelation to for the purpose of inspiration and bringing Glory to His Holy Name.

There are many who say that prophetic inspiration ended with the first Apostles of ADONAI when they died off, but that is contrary to the teachings of the Bible in which the Lord God spoke through the Apostle Paul; "*It was He (ADONAI) who gave gifts to people; He appointed some to be apostles, others to be prophets, others to be evangelists, others to be pastors and teachers. He did this to prepare all God's people for the work of Christian service, in order to build up the Body of Christ (ADONAI)"* (*Ephesians 4:11-13*). And again; *"He who speaks in a tongue edifies himself, but he who prophesies edifies the Church"* (*1Corinthians 14:4*). As well, the Apostle John claimed an inspiration from God about revealing the Truth throughout the Church Age for all Believers; *"But as for you, ADONAI has poured out His Spirit on you. As long as His Spirit remains in you, you do not need anyone to teach you. For His Spirit teaches you about everything, and what He teaches is true, not false. Obey the Spirit's teaching then and remain in union with ADONAI."* (*1John 2:26*)

Out of all the End-Times Prophecy, there are two distinct imageries that stand out as mysterious and controversial, and those are the references to the Beasts in Daniel 7:2-8, and the Dragon and Beast in Chapters 12, 13, 16 and 20 in the Book of Revelation. In the Book of Daniel, the Image which Daniel saw was of Four Beasts that represented four different kingdoms or governments that would be prominent on the earth, starting with the First Beast as Babylon, the Second Beast as the Medo-Persian's, the Third Beast would be Greece, and the Fourth Beast would be the Roman Empire. From the Fourth Beast will also come the End-Times Prophecy of the *"Last Days"* which will coincide with the Apostle John's Revelation. Daniel saw coming out the Fourth Beast, Ten Horns, which represents Ten Kingdoms that at that time will make up all the ruling governments of the world. Then he saw a Little Horn emerge and was given the heart of a man and had a mouth the spewed-out blasphemies. The Little Horn smites three of the Ten Horns and pulls them up by their roots (destroying them).

In the Book of Revelation, the Apostle John describes a vision of two Beasts. The first one he saw was coming out of the sea (which represents the Gentile Nations). It had Seven Heads, and Ten Horns with Crowns on each Horn. This symbolizes great Power and Authority, and the Ten Horns represent a Ten Nation Confederacy. This Beast (or Man) will be given all of the authority of Satan or in this representation the Great Dragon. This Man is known as the Antichrist. The Apostle Paul referred to him as "*The Man of Sin*" or "*The Son of Perdition*". He will be a boastful blasphemer insulting the Holy Beings of Heaven and the Lord God (ADONAI) Himself. He will be Satan incarnate and have the Powers of Darkness at his disposal.

He will broker a Peace Treaty with Israel and the rest of the world through this Ten Nation Confederacy and form a One World Government, One World Order, One World Religion, One World Monetary System (Currency).

This man will commit the ultimate blasphemy by making himself God (*Abomination of Desolation*) Matthew 24:15, when after the Third Temple is built in Jerusalem halfway through the Tribulation Period (1260 days), he will sit in the Holy Place and claim to be Messiah and Lord. Both the Prophet Daniel and Yeshua (ADONAI) spoke of this, and the horrible outcome as a result of his blasphemy. There is no turning back at this point.

83

After he enters into the Temple in Jerusalem and sits in the Holy Place, a subsequent event (sometime before the pouring out of the Bowls of God's Wrath, Revelation 16:1-21) of supernatural proportions will take place. Supernatural is that which defies the Laws of Nature (Laws of Physics) and the Physical Creation by means of circumventing its natural order by the Creator (God). The Taking Away or "*Rapture*" of the Church from the earth is this main event. The Dead in Christ (ADONAI) are raised first, then we (the Church still alive) are taken in a moment, transformed from physical flesh into spirit standing before ADONAI in Heaven, and given a new Eternal Body that is physical and will live forever.

So, the Church will go through the Minor portion and halfway through the Major portion of the Tribulation before the Taking Away occurs as mentioned by Yeshua in Matthew 24:15. This was not talking about, as most biblical scholars believed, the desecration of the 2nd Temple in Jerusalem by the Seleucid king Antiochus IV Epiphanes. This most certainly is referring to the End-Time event in the 3rd Temple when Yeshua is expounding on the Church of that time witnessing this event, prior to the Taking Away, which had not occurred yet.

There is also a counterpart to the First Beast, a Second Beast, he is the Antichrist's surrogate, the False Prophet; "*Then I saw another beast coming up out of the earth, and he had two horns like a lamb and spoke like a dragon. And he exercises all the authority of the First Beast in his presence and causes the earth and those that dwell in it to worship the First Beast...*"

(*Revelation 13:11-12*). There is also an "Image of the Beast" that the False Prophet brings to life, and it kills anyone that will not worship it. This undoubtedly is some kind of Artificial Intelligence (AI) that can replicate human speech and movement and has supernatural powers given to it by the Dragon (Satan).

The last thing the Antichrist and the False Prophet impose, is for all peoples of the earth (Small or Great, Rich or Poor, Free or Slave), to take a Mark of Allegiance to this Man and Image (on their forehead or right hand), referred to as "*The Mark of the Beast*", and no one may buy or sell anything without receiving the Mark. This is some kind of etching, tattoo, or micro-chip under the skin and cannot be removed. Once you take the Mark, you belong to the Dragon (Satan) and there are horrible repercussions for taking the Mark. So, there can be no counterfeit Mark as some believe you may be able to manufacture, for any replication of the Mark would be seen as Blasphemy by the Lord God (ADONAI), and a sincere heartfelt way to avoid persecution, which would be against the Will of God.

So, the precedent of the Two Beasts in Chapter 13 of the Book of Revelation, is in the event that is described in Chapter 12, where the Dragon (Satan) is finally and permanently cast out of Heaven; "*And war broke out in heaven: Michael and his angels fought with the dragon; and the dragon and his angels fought, but they did not prevail, nor was a place found for them in heaven any longer. So, the great dragon was cast out, that serpent of old, called the Devil and Satan, who deceives the whole world; he was cast to the earth, and his angels were cast out with him*" (*Revelation 12:7-9*). We must remember that Satan is a Liar (Father of all Lies), a Deceiver (Comes in the appearance of an Angel of Light), a Thief (he comes to Rob and Pillage), and a Destroyer and Murderer. In the form of the Beast, he attempts to overthrow the Lord God's Power, Sovereignty and Purpose. He tries once again to pretend that he can be like the Most High and turn what God has created as His Highest Order of Creation (Mankind) against Him and move it towards his evil preponderance.

There is no situation in which Evil will prevail over Good, that Unrighteousness will stand against Righteousness and win. It may appear that it does at times, especially with all of the wickedness and lawlessness upheaval all around us; but behind the scenes where the Spirit of God Reigns and all flesh is held accountable to, the Final Justice prevails and Good destroys Evil.

When God says that "My Ways are not your ways", He is saying in undeniable terms that we can never understand Him or completely see into His Mystery and Majesty, not even through an Eternity of being in His Presence. He is the Creator of all things and the Master and Majesty that Commands all things into being. There is no situation that He does not have Control or Dominion over. He is the Lord God, ADONAI, Yeshua, YAHWEH; and nothing in all of Heaven nor on the Earth can stand or prevail against His Will, **NOTHING!**

9

Suddenly it Comes Upon You
(Written in October 2013)

My Dearest Brethren, once again, the Lord (ADONAI) has given me something that I must share with you; two great visions that ADONAI has given me. It is something that I was allowed to witness and had a very brief participation in, but with everlasting impact and consequence. I can't give an exact amount of time involvement because this was something that ADONAI revealed outside the body, in Spirit, where these events are taking place right now. I am not the first person to ever have such a vision of this type or be part of its presentation, but I am bound by these two visions as they were given to me to reveal the truth to you all.

When ELOHIM reveals any part of His Purpose to mankind, the purpose behind it is to give mankind a view and insight into the Will of ADONAI, His Will for us, in order that He may be Glorified.

The first part of this vision (I don't know what else to call it), I believe is something that ADONAI is revealing to me alone, I have not in the last 44 years of my walk with Yeshua HaMashiach (Messiah) ever heard anyone speak of this vision before. It was a replay of something ADONAI showed me years ago, but this time its impact was so great I could barely contain my senses in front of it.

In the **First Vision**, I was standing in front of two tremendously large double-sided doors. It looked like they were made of cast iron with huge hinges on both sides from top to bottom. As I looked around, it looked like I was in a huge rock cave or cavern underground. Unlike the first time that "The Spirit" gave me this vision some years back, I could hear coming from behind the doors a loud thunderous roaring sound. All of a sudden, two large angels appeared standing at both doors ready to open them. Then a voice that sounded like thunder and the doors opened inward. As they opened the sight beyond them was both horrific and tremendous. It looked like an ocean of molten fire, churning like molten metal in a furnace. There was no heat coming from it, but I could sense the strong Presence of YAHWEH in the midst of it everywhere. I personally had no fear of it and I knew it was not a place that I was going to be entering into. The two angels were standing at the entrance blocking any entry that I could make. My desire was not to enter, but to witness its unbelievable immensity. I knew what it was I was looking at, but as I did the first time that ADONAI showed it to me, I asked, "What is this?" "The Spirit" answered, "*It is the Lake of Fire*". I replied, "the one you revealed to your Apostle?" and "The Spirit" answered, "*Yes*". Then "The Spirit" said to me, "*It has been prepared since before the foundations of the earth for Satan and his Fallen Angels. It is The Place of their Eternal Damnation.*" Then "The Spirit" reminded me that it is also the Second Death of the Final Judgement of YAHWEH, for all human beings who are found guilty of Blasphemy against the Word of YAHWEH and would not receive His Free Gift of Salvation.

As I stood gazing upon this Ocean of Fire, the shear knowledge of what I was gazing upon came to me, it is the Love of YAHWEH which is this Fire. The Love of YAHWEH, which is a Burning Fire and will be that substance of their torment forever and ever; as creatures of His Creation are totally made separated from any part of His Eternal Love and thrown into that Fire of His Love will burn and torment them from within, and without consuming them.

*   *   *   *   *

Then a **Second Vision** appeared to me; what looked like small individual cubed rooms, about four (4) feet by four (4) feet squared and maybe six feet tall, as far as you could see in all directions completely engulfed in darkness, but the darkness was not like here on earth, not like being in a completely dark closet and you couldn't see your hand in front of your face; it was the complete absence of any light, not the covering to shadow or restrict light from coming in, there was no light at all coming from any direction, inside or out. Beside me was an Angel of YAHWEH, but he did not say a word the whole time, just steadfast standing beside me. I believe it was the physical Presence of YAHWEH with me in order that I may survive and withstand being in the presence of this darkness (which was Death). What ADONAI was showing me (telling me) was that on earth (in the physical universe He has Created) the existence of all things comes directly from Him (which is Light) and all source of Light comes as a direct result of His Presence in all things Created. Wherever we are in the physical universe, there is light coming from every direction. Even when darkness intrudes on the source of light, there is consistent radiance existing. We can always come out of the darkness into the light, but in this place, it was spiritual darkness and transparency, I could see through it. It was like looking through a dark bluish-gray glass (crystal clear), with no radiance behind or in front of it. There were individuals (humans) inside these cubed rooms, and they were being inhibited from free form movement inside their space. They were all reacting to an internal (personal) torment, like they were insane and in great anguish, some thrashing around wailing and others holding their heads screaming continuously and beating themselves. I was in close proximity at times to them, and could clearly see them, but they could not see me. I asked ADONAI how this was; and "The Spirit" told me that I was among the living, and these were among the dead. Their torment is the result of their total separation from YAHWEH. I asked ADONAI, how could they be totally separated from YAHWEH, who made that decision; "The Spirit" answered me sternly, "*THEY made that decision!*" At that moment, everything shook, and I could see every person falling to their knees trembling in fear. It felt like a double-edged sword had gone through me, then out of me again. It was the Word of YAHWEH speaking (ADONAI).

ADONAI spoke one more thing to me before taking me out of that place; "The Spirit" revealed what I was witnessing and where this place was; it is the darkness that is inside every human being, the holding place where YAHWEH has separated the Darkness from the

90

Light. It is the Grave [Sheol], it is Death, and the captive place of bondage before the Final Day of Judgement (Revelation 20:11-15); and it is more real than anything we have experienced in our human physical life on earth.

ADONAI made it quite clear, that this is not what He intended for Mankind; this is not what His Heart desired for us. This is a willful desire of the individuals here to reject the Free Gift of Salvation that ELOHIM has provided to every person ever conceived and born. It is the final outcome of their blasphemous and arrogant lives, where now, right at this moment, they are in complete and utter Eternal Darkness and fear and torment; not torment like being hung and having your flesh ripped apart from your body kind of torment, but fear that is so intense and completely incarcerating that it engulfs every molecule of your being. There is no goodness or love or satisfaction of any kind in the midst of the pain and anguish which is being suffered without substance of time, continuous and unceasing with no hope of any end in sight. This is what death has brought onto them, not an end to all things, but the everlasting beginning of unending torment. This is the outcome of complete and total separation from YAHWEH and the attributes you shared while you were alive in your body as a human being on earth. There is no word in any language that can begin to describe the kind of fear which leads to utter torment like this is.

It must be totally understood that YAHWEH has completely and everlastingly provided a "way out" to this kind of end for each and every person who has ever been born. YAHWEH does not send anyone to Eternal Darkness and Damnation; they condemn themselves to it.

ADONAI is not a statue or piece of jewelry you wear or icon you have hanging from your rear-view mirror.

ADONAI is not a philosophy or religion or good feeling which comes and goes at our pleasure.

ADONAI is not everything around us, He is the Creator of all things. There is only One God.

ADONAI is not an unseen force that exists throughout the universe and has no interaction with us.

ADONAI is Holy, He is the only One who is Holy.

ADONAI is Love and He is Spirit.

ADONAI is Eternal, He has No Beginning, and He has No End; He was not Created, He is the Creator. He is the Judge of All of His Creation, He is YAHWEH!

As "The Spirit" commands it to be revealed, there is only One God and He has revealed Himself to His Creation as One God; Father (ABBA), Son (Yeshua HaMashiach) and Holy Spirit (Ruach HaKodesh), One in the Same (ELOHIM). He has revealed Himself to all of mankind without exception as the Savior of Mankind; as the Son of God; as the Son of
Man; as The Father to His Children who will receive Him as such; as Yeshua HaMashiach, The King of Kings and The Lord of Lords.

**Make no mistake of it,
He is ADONAI and He is ELOHIM!**
(Lord and God)

10

The Virtues of God
(Written in March 2021)

Shalom…from Ken, an Elder in the Church, who by Faith has been called by the Great God and Saviour, Jesus (Yeshua) the Lord (*ADONAI*), to be a Believer and Teacher for the edification of the Believers of the Way, the Church or Body of Messiah. I am led by the Holy Spirit (*Ruach HaKodesh*) to write you and reveal what the Lord God (*ADONAI*) is saying…

We (*Human Beings*) are the highest order of creation, for we are all created in the image of God. We are the only part of the creation (*both in Heaven and the physical universe*) whereby Faith can be exercised, and therefore the act of Faith be honoured as an expression to the true Nature and Will of God the Father. Only mankind has been given the act of exercising Faith…it is the essence of an expression given from the spirit of man (heartfelt) unto the presence of God the Father. It has been given by order of God that all creation have a free will of choice; but because of our unique position within the creation, we are given the right to express Faith as an act of worship and covenant with God.

Out of the three (3) Virtues of God (Faith, Hope and Love) Hope and Love can only be expressed through the act of Faith. Even though Love is the greatest virtue, it cannot be expressed without the act of Faith. Faith is the greatest single act a Human Being can give towards God. The beginning of our salvation is through the act of <u>Faith</u>… Faith in Jesus Christ! "*For God so loved* the world, that He *gave* his only Begotten Son, so that whoever *believes* in Him should not perish but have Eternal Life...for whomever *believes* in the Son of God has Eternal Life". In this testimony God shows that Love is the greatest virtue, and that His giving is the Hope, whereby our act of Faith in believing is when we receive Eternal Life. It shows that God loved us first, then we, through our expression of Faith received and loved Him back. Nevertheless, the expression of Faith we exercise must be equal to the Nature of God's expression of Faith. In order for our Faith to be received by God so that He may act upon it and give honour unto Himself through it, our Faith must be expressed within the virtue that God expresses it. The way in which God expresses the virtue of Faith is without *Any Doubt*. The mystery in this, is that God honours Himself through the act of a Virtue which expresses the essence of His Holiness.

The essence of God is felt throughout the physical universe; but the presence of God is extended from Heaven (Spirit) to the earth through mankind. Therefore, the Presence of God stands before mankind and the Spirit of God comes through mankind by the Virtue of Faith in Jesus the Christ (ADONAI), which is given to us through the Virtue of Love from God the Father. Faith is the kinetic energy that enables us to request and receive ALL things from God, He reacts to the Virtue of Faith which has *No Doubt* in both requesting and receiving.

In the scheme of Creation, there is One Thing that God has endorsed as an absolute point of worship, and that is <u>Praise</u>. In the Psalms both King David and his son Solomon expounded on Praise as being the highest order of worship, and throughout the Bible, Praise is a constant reminder of God's pleasure with His people. In the purest sense of how God expresses His desire for us to Praise Him, it is based on Righteousness directed towards Him out of an expression from our hearts through the Virtue of Faith. Where we give and He receives, when our spirit literally joins with God's Spirit through an act He has designated as being Holy and Righteous and can only be linked by Faith. Because God knows the hearts of all men, He set NO restrictions on how mankind would Praise Him. No act of true expression has been forbidden. When God established His first Covenant with His people (Israel) it was based on strict adherence to the rituals and physical tasks laid out in the Law (*Torah*) that God had given through Moses. Worship in its purest form came by way of obedience and strict following to the Law of Moses. It was based around offerings and sacrifices ranging from Tithe Offerings to Burnt Animal Sacrifices. It was not based on Faith (for nothing in the Law is based on Faith) but upon Obedience. [Command and requirement (God) > obedience and fulfillment (Man)]. The outcome [Reward or Punishment] became the foundation for the social standards by which we (all mankind) would base our cultural institutions and laws.

Throughout our histories, mankind has mischaracterized what God has demonstrated and relayed as a Holy Virtue (Faith) and turned it into a man-made virtue based around the outcome of obedience to the Law. We institutionalize every aspect of our existence. We flatter ourselves with degrees of education and call it knowledge. We adorn the wisdom of leadership who self-sacrifice, long study, endure hardship and live in solitude and call that Godly. What was given by God as a Virtue through His Spirit to mankind, is turned into dogma, rituals, and pride. Because mankind is in a fallen state with God, we are engulfed with a sin consciousness as a natural mental state of Being, therefore we equate 'Good Works' with Holy Deeds. These become self-righteous acts, which perpetrate more and more ritual and eventually become spiritual (religious) in order to satisfy unresolved mysteries of our existence. As these evolve through social evolution (customs and culture) fulfillment of dogma and ritual becomes a substitute for Faith, and that which is tangible (physical creation) becomes the point of focus for worship. The result becomes blasphemy in the Sight of God because the Virtue of Faith, which requires no physical evidence of God for worship, has been replaced by the need to produce a physical image or icon in order to worship. Case in point, as decreed by God through His written testimony within the Bible, "*Faith comes by hearing and hearing by the Word of God*". There is NO substitution for the Virtue of Faith in order to fulfill the Will of God. It is based on the principle and fact that what is unseen (Spirit) created all things that can be seen (Physical Universe) and was done through a Command by the Creator (God) as the result of Faith (*without any Doubt*).

Our physical worship towards God must be in regard to the inner sanctuary of our Faith. The physical Temple of

God, which stores both His Spirit and the Covenant, is our physical body once we receive Salvation through Jesus the Christ and are Born Again. There are only three (3) outward signs of this happening; 1) our Confession as being a sinner, 2) our Baptism (through the Holy Spirit), 3) our Testimony in Faith. The redemption of our Being is unseen (Spirit) but the manifestation of it is through the testimony we project as a living witness through the Virtue of Faith in Jesus (Yeshua *ADONAI*).

As humans are born into a fallen state, our flesh (body) has had control over the emotions and character of our Being. There is transference of this character into our redeemed state because of the free will God has empowered us with. Our quest to be right with God can in many instances create situations which overindulge our desire to stand in Faith, thus what should be developing into a state of righteousness through Faith, develops into acts of self-righteousness through pride. The typical scenario for this is in the assembly of Believers where pride enters into acts of worship. There is an oblique result and outcome that relates to the overt physical displays of sensational emotionalism given when people come together in open forums of worship towards God, especially if a T.V. camera is in front of them. The Sunday morning worship service becomes the Broadway Production which keeps them coming back week after week…it's the hour of entertainment and production, not the 30 minutes of prepared speech afterwards that makes the Sunday Mornings worth getting all dressed up for. Notice too, that not only is Tithing a constant reminder to the assembly faithful by means of guilt (using verses of Scripture as commands of obedience); but the shear elegance and social stance of the production and the facility hit an accord with pride and ego for one to sustain such a holy cause. The bottom-line is that the Church is "Big Business" and a "Social Status" Icon, and the order of business is made quite clear in the ritual and process. The first hour is spent enjoying either a well-rehearsed musical production or drama production (or both), in most cases usually followed by a solo act (vocalist or musician), then church business and social announcements, then it's time to pay, the "Offering" is taken (*the term Offering or Tithing legally maintains the standing of a Not for Profit or Non-Profit Organization with the IRS...so does the term Donations*), any place else for such a social event you'd have to buy a Ticket (*which would be considered Income and taxable*). If the Offerings have not been as high as the projected budget forecast, then the Pastor or chosen announcer will give a stern reminder that God demands our Tithing, and in not doing so means we are cheating God out of what is His...sometimes in frustration they'll mention that nothing is free, and our donations pay the bills and keeps the building projects going. What that means from a corporate sense: this buys more land and buildings which the church corporation owns and controls; and pays the salaries for the full-time staff (Pastor, Secretary, Business Manager, Associate Pastor, Youth Pastor, and Facility Maintenance), and all publications and printing. If the ministry is a T.V. or Radio production, then there is the cost involved with full support of that as well and in most instances the cost associated with this is more intense than the basic pastoral church service. Once all the business aspects have been taken care of, then comes the sermon or message, which is usually regimented to a strict 30-minute allotment. Then it's over and everyone somehow feels a fulfillment of obligation as a holy deed towards God. The inference here is in creating a Corporate Church and Religious Institution based on Dogmatic Rituals and Carnality which resembles the appearance of holiness; but produces Pandemonium, far removed from the Virtue of Faith, and has allowed the Church to prophetically fulfill its place in the Last Days of the End-Times as the Church of Laodicea *(Revelation 3:14-21)*.

Sadly, the Church of Laodicea is the Church (*Body of Christ*) in this present dispensation, a Lukewarm condition produced because of a rejection of Faith but an adherence to satisfying the flesh (*with an outward appearance of holiness but within all corruption and dead man's bones*), and because of it the Lord will spit this Church out of His mouth...He will reject the Corporate Church, He will reject Religious Institutions, He will reject the pandemonium and those who oppress Faith, He will reject the Proud and Boastful even if they claim it in the Name of the Lord from the Pulpit, and He will reject the man-made institution of the Church which in their greed and self-indulgence place a burden of guilt in trying to control the faithfulness of Tithes and Offerings. Thus says the Lord, "*I will reject those who have demanded Tithing and laid a burden of oppression upon My Namesake, for I the Lord have asked each man to come before my table with a clean and open* heart of sacrifice. The gift of burden is not welcomed to be placed at my door!", thus says the Lord God. The absolute result of our actions only satisfies our flesh and cardinality if it is not exercised from the heart (spirit) and soul (mind) enacted through the Virtue of Faith. God is worthy to be Praised and Glorified. The first and most precious commandment of God is to Love the Lord your God above All things...with all of your body (flesh), soul (mind) and heart (spirit). Once again, God has empowered us with the Virtue of His own Holiness and a command He set forth which is sustained, to this very moment by His own Will, through unwavering Faith (without doubt). ALL flesh (Creation) is corrupted and in the Sight of God is sin. The soul (mind) is the central control point of the Human Being. It is fed constantly with information and emotions from either the desires of the flesh (sin) or of the heart (spirit). The mind determines how the Human Being will react to the information and emotions from these two sources. The desires of the flesh are outside of the Virtues which God has established through Faith. The flesh is outside of the Perfect Will of God because from inception the first Human Being (Adam) was transformed into sin because of his own desire to follow his flesh through an act of disobedience and blasphemy. Sin engulfed and morphed his entire being (body, soul and spirit), from the highest level of creation in perfection (standing in the Presence of God), to the highest level of creation in a fallen state (separated from the Presence of God).

Therefore, how should we act as a renewed creature and follower of Jesus (Yeshua Adonai). The only answer that God will accept and not bring before His Judgment is FAITH *(without any Doubt).* It's not found in going to Church, for WE who are in Jesus (Yeshua Adonai) are the Church, and as a collective assembly of Believers we are His Body *(the Body of Christ).* Adonai told us to not forbid ourselves from assembling together for the purpose of worshiping God, but rather He commanded us to go throughout ALL of the earth and proclaim the 'Good News' that He has risen from death and sits at the Right Hand of the Father, for He is Lord and God (ADONAI)...that HE brings salvation to Everyone who will call upon His Name and believe in Him, and that if anyone will do this, they will have Life Eternal! The Lord DID NOT mean for us to become complacent in our testimony of this 'Good News' so that we end up in the assembly gathered together only and not doing the proclaiming throughout the earth. As a collective worldwide body, the Lord has established leadership by way of callings (Ephesians 4:11-12) to build the Body Assembly into individual living testimonies, which shall proclaim the 'Good News' about Jesus (Yeshua *Adonai*). Our regard should not be to go to church each Sunday and put in an hour or two, hear a prepared speech regarding some bible history or political/social context, and then go to lunch. Our assemblage should be for worship and in order for the Church Leadership to boost our Faith and direct us in the Ways of the Spirit who teaches us ALL Things (*1John 2:26-27*) so that we may be a living witness for the Lord at all times.

The caveat to all of this is FAITH (*without any Doubt*)...Nothing can be requested, received or executed without Faith. The Lord God holds EACH person accountable for their actions according to their Faith. No one will be standing before the Lord in righteousness, inexcusable of sin because they went to church regularly or was a Church Member, or because they paid tithes and gave offerings, or gave regularly to a TV Evangelist, or because they handed out food at a mission during a holiday season, or because of... Anything Except FAITH! ...in Jesus the Christ! (ADONAI) AMEN.

-11-
Warning Against Blasphemy
(Written in August 2006)

Take this as a friendly and loving gesture; but one of stern warning from the Spirit of God.

Blasphemy comes in many different forms and for many different reasons. Sometimes it's because the person saying the blasphemy isn't aware that it is such an act. Other times it is a deliberate action of total disregard towards God in His Majesty and Glory. Many people have such hatred towards God that they love saying things that demeanor Him and willfully continue to do so repeatedly on any occasion. In many instances, the blasphemy is just part of the person's profanity, what they would consider a phrase which is not bad cursing or insulting to others, mildly affective in releasing their frustrations.

In the Written Word of God (The Bible), The Lord gave mankind His Law by which He holds all people accountable from the time His Angel gave them to Moses. A Covenant between God and his Chosen People was made with Abraham and passed to Moses under the Law of Sanctification and is binding forever. It, the Law (*Torah*) lets man forever know that in his flesh is a constant and unforgiving state of sin. It is the outcome of man's disobedience towards God from the very beginning of man's free-standing and rebellious nature and continues to this very day. This (*Torah*), called ADONAI's Mitzvah (Ten Commandments), are reflective of the general nature of God's Will for man to always be in tune and obedient too. It is and will be the major part of what God judges a person against (His Standard) when He Judges all of the human creation at the Great White Throne Judgment (Revelation 20:11-15).

The 3rd of these Ten Commandment states; "*Do not use My Name in Vain (for evil purposes), for I, the Lord your God (ADONAI), will punish anyone who misuses My Name*."

In this complete context, the reference to "*My Name*" is the only identity God makes to His Being, and the Majesty of His Holiness. The only thing His People had was a term used from the original reference that He gave Moses as to who He was when Moses asked The Lord; "*who shall I tell the people sent me?*", and the Lord's answer to Moses was, "I AM that I AM! Tell them therefore that I AM sent you." (Exodus 3:14). Because God was reverenced above all things and could not be equated to anything that man could conceive, this word "I AM" in Hebrew given by God was a specific Name which translates in their tongue as *YAHWEH* (four Hebrew Consonants 'YHWH' Yod, Hey, Vav, Hey - YaHaVah), this is God's sacred, personal name (Extremely Holy). It expresses His Essence and Personality to His Creation. The Letters comprise a word that would transliterate into "*The Sovereign Lord*" or "*The Lord*". It was so Holy that no one could write or speak it, therefore another word had to be devised which would make up the essence of the transliterated vowels and could be spoken and used by the common man. This became *ADONAI* (the Lord God). When the four consonants of *YAHWEH* were to be written down in text as Scripture, the word *ADONAI was* used, only chosen Scribes from the Tribe of Levi could be the text writer, and they had to completely wash themselves each time before scribing the four Consonants. The context of the 3rd Commandment was intended and understood to be that Holy.

The Law was not meant to cleanse man from his sin; but rather to remind man of his sin and that he needed God to constantly forgive him. This was accomplished through the Law's mandatory processes of temporary redemption and cleansing through ritual performances and a stand-in replicate (the Temple) and earthly representative of God (the High Priest). All of this was to remind and demonstrate the Holy Nature and Being of God and how far out of reach man truly was with Him. Only through temporal means could man be in somewhat good standing with God and not be killed or destroyed by God Himself. Without the Temple and the Law, there was no representative for man with God. Nothing could reach, touch or commune with God at the level of his Holiness except through these means, and nothing was able to please God in His forgiveness of man's disobedience, nor the retraction of His curse against man which was Death due to the act of sin and the nature of sin in all man's flesh.

The term *ADONAI* was not what God would give to man as a possession of His Name or the essence of His Mercy towards man. That would be for a later time, under a New Covenant that the Lord God, as the image of "The Father" (ABBA YAHWEH), would give to all mankind, through the Priestly and Royal Line of His Chosen People and establish His Name forever.

105

The importance of God establishing His Name with Mankind was to give man a means of approaching His Holiness and receive both Mercy and Forgiveness in a permanent way. Unlike man where our names identify us to three dimensional characteristics and give us recognizable individuality; God is Spirit and beyond the dimensional characteristics of our human senses. From the very beginning when the Lord God created all things, both in Heaven and the physical universe, He did so by taking a vow unto His Own Name and commanded them into being through His Word. "The Word" was in fact one-in-the-same as Himself (Elohim), the complete essence of God in Spirit and Being.

It is through "The Word" that everything was created and how all substance which is physical (seen and unseen) came into being. It is through "The Word" that God would fulfill the promises of the First Covenant with Abraham and reconcile mankind unto Himself from the bondage of sin and condemnation of the Law. It is through "The Word" that God revealed His Holy and Eternal Name and would sanctify all mankind unto Himself and bridge the gap between death and His Holiness and afford man Eternal Life. God bridged that gap by sending us "The Word" in the form of a man (the God Man) who would give us that Eternal Life through His Name and be the only sacrifice that would be fulfilling and completely sanctified unto God as a sacrifice worthy of His Sin Offering in accordance with His Law.

"In the beginning was The Word, and The Word was with God, and The Word was God!" (John 1:1-3). "The Word" became flesh and was given to us as the Son of God and

His Name would be the only source of our forgiveness. So Holy is His Name, that it is above all things in Heaven and on Earth and in the Underworld. He sits at the Right Hand of the Power of God (The Father) and is the Judge of all mankind.

God has declared that His Son be the Savior of the world and that His Name is the only source of power which can call upon The Father in fulfilling the Will of God. The Name of the Son of God is the fulfillment of the 3rd Commandment of God. The Name of the Son of God is Jesus (*Yeshua*), the Christ (HaMashiach), who is Lord and God (1John 5:19-20).

Any use of this Name other than to Praise, Honor or Glorify God is indeed a blasphemy and requires the individual who is dishonoring it to consider the profound context of judgment ruling against them.

"For God so loved the world that He gave his only begotten Son, so that whomsoever should believe in Him (His Name), should not die but have Eternal Life." (John 3:16)

And Jesus said, *"I will do whatever you ask for in My Name, so that the Father's Glory will be shown through the Son. If you ask me for anything in My Name, I will do it."* (John 14:13-14)

Please consider this the next time you choose a name or a phrase to expound your profanity or release unconscious frustration openly.

The Resulting Sound of God
(Written in July 2000)

*From Ken, who is an elder within the Church, this is my eyewitness testimony and what the Spirit of God has given me to reveal to the world, according to what I have seen and been given as a witness of what God has prepared for those who Love Him! In Yeshua ADONAI, who is the **King of Kings** and the **Lord of Lords**, He is the One who sits on the Throne of God (Elohim) at the Right Hand of the Father and has revealed these things through the Spirit (Ruach HaKodesh), to His imperfect servant who loves Him so that He may receive Glory and Honour, AMEN.*

In Heaven, you are in the complete and unrestricted Abode of God. It is not only where He Reigns from, but where His Power originates from. You are immediately aware of His Presence in everything, and your mind is so clear that you can concentrate on as many things as you wish and each thing is as if it is the only thing you are concentrating on, yet you may be concentrating on many things at the same time with full cognizant understanding of all these things. Your entire being is set on Faith and there is not a bit of doubt in what you are seeing or thinking nor anything around you or inside of you, Faith is the focus and the force that is Majesty in Heaven.

This is what it is like, this is what it will be like once God brings All Things back unto Himself and we are standing before the Almighty in our New Body (Resurrected Being). You are aware of everything and everyone you meet; you know their names and feel that you have always known them. When gazing upon the Throne of God, all of your senses witness the absolute and Unconditional Love that emanates through every molecule of your being, down to the atomic level in a manner and way that has never been expressed or seen in your existence or experience while living in human form on the earth. There is no sin or consciousness of evil to object to God's Love or interfere with the Will of God. There is no Adversary or tempting forces opposing God's Eternal Love and Perfection.

There is a calm stillness and serenity of peace which engulfs you and is within the atmosphere and all through the environment in every direction going to infinity. From the Throne of God, His Light is permeating through all that He has created. There is no darkness, there are no shadows hiding behind anything, just pure light, pure energy and pure force radiating in all directions coming out of everything; the ground, the sky, the clouds, the flowers, the trees, every creature you see, the mountains, the water, the streets, the fruit on the trees, any structures or buildings, everything!

Within the stillness and peaceful serenity, you feel and hear a vibration which is coming from the Light that is emanating out of everything and coming from every direction. It is the Resulting Sound of God's Glory singing forth and is a beautiful meditating and surreal sound. It is indeed glorious and brings forth the Peaceful Serenity you feel. You are constantly surrounded by light and sound, but never to the point of confusion or your inability to withstand His intensity. There is also unbelievable music, like you've never heard before and the sounds of beautifully orchestrated melody which seems to have no beginning and no end and fits the surrounding situation you are in at the moment. It follows you were ever you go, but there is no sense of origination or volume, just peaceful and perfect. There is no aggravation or annoyance of any kind, nothing is too repetitious or boring. Things appear and you move through panoramic scenes of unspeakable beauty and pageantry.

You have your five senses (sight, hearing, taste, smell and feeling), but these are purely enhanced beyond your human created state. You also have other senses and abilities which are unhuman that I cannot describe to you through this sinful flesh.

There are so many new things manifested before you that you've ever seen or imagined on Earth. Things that could only be in Heaven where the Holiness of God's Perfect Will exists; things that cannot be in the presence of sin, which God cannot manifest on Earth because of the sin which exists there. You can sense the absence of time but are aware of Eternal Existence. The mere fact that you can gaze upon the Throne of God and see His Image without any restriction gives you a complete sense of security that you shall live forever. Everything emanates Love and Peace which completely surrounds you Eternally. You are totally and completely aware of where this Love and Peace is coming from, it is the One who sits on the Throne and is called the **Holy of Holies**. Nothing is without Praise towards God, everything and everyone is constantly and willfully Praising and Worshiping the One who sits on the Throne. He is constantly speaking and conveying the Word of God and His Oracles to all of His Creation. His Voice is like substance that fills your starving hunger and satisfies an unquenchable thirst. There is no want or care, no need for a request or supplication; no condemnation or repentance, no judgments or injustice, no crying or remorse, no laws or restriction, no revelations or prophecies, there is no doubt or questions to be answered; just pure substance of Truth and Unconditional Love…Utter Holiness!

The communication in Heaven between God and His creation is through Faith and manifested by His Spirit. The Mind of God and the Being of God are one in the same and there are no restrictions in receiving ALL Things in Righteousness, no guilt of unworthiness or doubt. You cannot see the beginning or the end of anything; there is no birth or death any longer. Everything is as God is, Eternal! You see and witness the true Essence of God and He fills everything with His Radiance and Love, which is His Radiance and His Glory. God does not make you worship Him; you want to worship Him! Every fiber of your being is in Love with Him, and your uncontrollable desire is to worship Him. Everything and everyone in Heaven are constantly worshiping God and it is the most beautiful sight to behold Forever and Ever! Amen.

-13-
How Powerful is the Truth?
(Written in August 2020)

Is it enough to just Know the Truth?

Is it enough to just Believe in the Truth?

Is it enough to Work within and for the Truth?

The **Truth** is so powerful that it made all things in Heaven and in the physical universe; and He set forth the Command which is still going forward for all these things to exist and remain in existence.

The Truth is not human; it is not carnal but rather Spirit.

The Truth became flesh and lived among us and is the very Essence of God.

The Truth created all things that are visible and invisible.

The Truth cannot substantiate a lie, nor have any fellowship with a liar.

The Truth had no beginning and has no end, He is Holy, Eternal and is God.

But you say:

I thought God was *Love.*

I thought God was *Grace.*

I thought God was *Mercy.*

I thought God was All Powerful.

These are ALL the Things that make up what God is to His Creation, but the Truth is what makes every Human Being hunger for God, and quenches that unquenchable thirst for knowledge and wisdom.

Truth is the reality of Christ, and under Him comes the basis for all Truth; and this Truth is Eternal Life and Everlasting Peace.

When the Lord says that "*My Ways are not your ways*", and that He is above us in ALL manner of being; we do not comprehend that it means He is incomprehensible to us. To be Above your Ways means that you are not at the same level; that you do not share in totality with Him, that you cannot ever comprehend the True Essence of God, that even given an Eternity of gazing upon His Glory, we will never be able to absorb or see the completeness of God in any manner. He is Holy, without any beginning and has always been the **Great I AM**. When Moses asked the Lord God Almighty, "who do I tell the people sent me to them? They will ask, what is His Name? What shall I say to them? And the Lord God answered Moses, "*I AM WHO I AM*", and He said, "*Thus, you shall say to the children of Israel, I AM has sent me to you*."

The Lord has shown me, that we have made no cornerstone to anything that stands Forever; no foundation that anything can stand upon and not crumble or be destroyed. We have not prepared a place that God can Live in our Midst from Everlasting to Everlasting. We have no power to shape the universe into what it is for His Pleasure, nor Created the Earth as His Footstool; but it is He who has done all these things; and He has brought forth ALL Life in Heaven and on Earth. All things seen, and unseen came from Him and were within Him before there was a Beginning of All Things.

There is no vernacular in all of Creation that can describe or justify the Greatness of God and His Holiness. Not even the *Glorious Beings* that surround the Throne of the Living God have understanding of the Greatness and Eternal Wonder of God, yet they pronounced Him as "Holy, Holy, Holy is the Lord God Almighty!"

God has revealed His Shekinah to His Creation, where the Spirit becomes the physical evidence of God's Glorious Presence.

Abraham witnessed it when the Presence of the Lord came down upon Sodom and Gomorrah and passed Judgement against them. Moses saw it in a Bush that Burned like a fiery torch but was not consumed and the Thunderous Voice that came from the Fiery Cloud that surrounded the mountain of God; he saw the fiery finger that carved out the words in stone as the Commandments of God on Mount Sinai. The Children of Israel witnessed it for forty years wandering in the desert, as the Presence of God in a Cloud that hovered over them by day and a Fiery Torch that surrounded their encampment at night. Shadrach, Meshach and Abednego witnessed it when the Lord appeared in the midst of the fiery furnace they had been thrown into and saved them from being burned up alive. Elijah saw it when the Fiery Presence of God came down and consumed and received his Offerings to the Lord, over those of the prophets of Baal. The Apostles saw it with the Transfiguration when the Shekinah came upon and through Yeshua on the mountain. The two Roman Soldiers saw it when the Son of God stepped out of death and into Life and the Presence of God shown brighter than the sun in the midst of His Crucifixion Tomb. Saul of Tarsus saw it on the road to Damascus when Yeshua appeared to him as a Fiery Light brighter than the Mid-Day sun. The Apostles and many witnesses saw it on the Day of Pentecost, when the Holy Spirit was given back to mankind and the Glory of God came upon their heads and the Secret Truths about God were now being revealed.

As humans we are born into sin, our minds are constantly filled with humanistic doubt, and we are encapsulated in the five senses of our being. It is indeed a miracle that any of us ever receive Yeshua ADONAI into our hearts and the knowledge of the Truth be received into our conscience minds.

There is not enough good works or positive motivation that any one of us can do to put a crown of glory on our heads. Not in a lifetime of service towards any measure of charity or the amount of giving of one's own wealth can this appease the nature of our sinful character in the Eyes of God. We are accepted by God not because of our "Good Deeds" and works, but in spite of them. For what we do in our human ability, in our fallen state of sin, is but filthy rags in the Eyes of ADONAI.

Belief in something does not circumvent the Truth.

Wishing you well or passing along positive thoughts

and energy to someone does not impart the power that will Command these things into reality. The cosmic energy of the universe is not the Divine Presence of God and the idea that humans control their own salvation, and destiny is a Lie. YAHWEH has given each and every human born a "Free-Will". This sets man above the other creatures on this planet to interface with the Creation and with God without restriction. It also determines the outcome of each human being born as to their pathway and destiny in this life and into Eternity.

The truth is all humans are Spirit Beings having a temporal physical Human Experience. We are Eternal Beings made in the Image of God, and God has chosen that we have a physical form (Body) which will also be Eternal. YAHWEH has determined that this pathway into our Eternal Being will travel on only one of two directions. Either into His Eternal and Glorious Presence through the Salvation that He has provided or towards Eternal Damnation as the result of His Holy Judgement against the Blasphemy of not receiving His Free Gift of Salvation. Either way, it is determined by the Free-Will that God has given each of us; we make that decision for ourselves. God's Will is that no person goes into the Judgement that leads to damnation but receive the Free Gift of Eternal Life through Yeshua ADONAI.

The assumption that to Live for ADONAI is to live in total disobedience to the Flesh, is a distraction away from the Truth. We can in no way shed our sin nature, just as we can in no way shed our skin. It is part of our inherent being, born into sin, and must be transformed into a new being (Born Again) by the Redemptive Power of God, through Yeshua ADONAI.

ADONAI has declared His Presence through everything that He has Created and has set His Standard for all things to go forth in Perpetuity. God has only sanctioned man the ability to reproduce what He (God) has created in Righteousness. Each species reproduces after its own kind. He has not sanctioned our manipulation of the creation to our desire or science in order to pervert any form of it to our liking or invention. To take the natural order of what has been created by God and change it into something unnatural is an abomination and a perversion which will fall under His Judgement and Wrath. Woe to all who fall under His Wrath, for God will not be mocked, nor is the Truth to be made into a lie!

14

On Your Knees
(Written in May 2019)

This is the testimony of what The Lord God (ADONAI) has purposed through His imperfect servant, in order that what He has shown may be made a credible witness to His Majesty and Holiness.

I am writing this out of great love, admiration and respect for the Most High, for He is divulging His Holy Purpose behind creating us (Humankind) as an extension of Himself, as His Highest Order of Creation. What the Spirit reveals to us is the residue of His Holiness and the Force of His Divine Power. He nurtures our Faith and becomes Life itself - *Adonai Eloheinu Adonai Echad. He is the Sovereign Lord God Almighty and there is no other god beside Him; there is no other! Amen.*

In the midst of a recent and very painful injury, ADONAI has given to me that the place to be is "On Your knees". Like anyone who was looking to ADONAI for both help and understanding on why such an excruciating thing had to occur, the Ruach HaKodesh (Holy Spirit) led me away from why God allowed it to happen and moved me towards the revelation on how this event and my painful suffering was intended to give me the opportunity to worship God in a fashion that would humble me as His Servant and bring Great Glory to His Name. Now, let me make it quite clear that I am not a masochist, nor a flagellant and I have never before used pain as a means to exhort myself towards worshiping God at a higher level of exaltation.

This was without doubt, an accident that I brought about by my own fruition, but according to God's perfect timing was given to me as a means to demonstrate His Perfect Love. The opportunity for me to exercise Unquestionable Faith and to be humbled so that Faith would produce Worship in the truest and most purest form. This was not being perpetrated to punish me or chastise me. It was not God showing His Absolute Authority and Over-Handedness regarding any sinful nature that still existed in me or in my life. But instead, it was a show of His Great Love, Perfection and Oversight to bestow upon me an opportunity to Worship Him without any reservation or doubt as to His Supreme Majesty and Holiness.

I could tell that I was being approached by Him as a Renewed Creature, one that complete propitiation had been given to. It revealed to me that God is always with us, with those that Love Him. That He cares for us beyond any understanding that we can imagine. It was a cleansing of my Worship and an honour to see God as He really is, Faithful and True to His Word! But and there is a "but" in this scenario, **He is Holy!** Far, far removed from anything that we can understand or equate too. His Ways are most definitely not our ways, for He is the Lord God Almighty, Holy, and far above all things that we can see or imagine.

The Voice of ADONAI came to me at that very moment in which I was immobilized and in great agony and hit the very depth of my spirit with Absolution, Mercy, Hope and a sense of His Holy Unwavering Love. At this moment when I was ready to call out to ADONAI for help, instead The Word said to me, "*On Your knees*". I immediately took it as a Revelation, and I knew exactly what *Ruach HaKodesh* was saying to me as well as everything else He would say. "*On Your knees*" is a show of absolute Humility, Respect and Surrender to the Will of God. It is not, nor should it ever be looked upon or revered as a human expression of protest or disobedience against authority.

As ADONAI was showing me His Love, I could feel myself giving into His Will through my Humility. The more I gave into humbling myself before ADONAI and outward worshiping Him, the more I could feel His Love towards me and this upheaval of love and respect inside of me for Him like I had never before. The more I concentrated on Him and the less I concentrated on myself, then I realized the true meaning of what Yeshua had said, "*Seek ye first the Kingdom of God, and His Righteousness; and all these things shall follow*." (Matthew 6:33) The "all these things shall follow" are the issues we have in our human life (the desires and needs we are constantly bringing before God).

The deception that the modern Church in this dispensation (Laodicea) has been perpetrating and promoting as Believers, is that God is a "Fix It All" kind of image, one who will give us the desires of our hearts if we only believe in Him and try not to sin any longer. In our thoughts and self-righteous attempts, hopefully we are praying the right way, saying it the right way and not asking too many selfish desires, but asking enough to get what we want. In many instances, the focus and point of desires is totally on "us" and not on God. The whole purpose for even believing in God is to bring about maximum benefit for "us". This is the evil selfishness of our flesh and the desire to call God at will to serve us, instead of recognizing that He is the Lord, and we are to be the servant. The image that the church loves to use of Yeshua from the written word (Gospels) is that Yeshua projected Himself as a Servant to us. This of course is not the image that God ever projected Himself from Heaven, which is where Yeshua is Sitting at the Right Hand of the Power of God. He is not the humble servant acting in a human capacity showing us how to be humble, but rather, He is the King of Kings and the Lord of Lords. His face is brighter than the sun and He radiates Glory from His Being in all directions. When he speaks, all of Heaven falls to His Majesty and when He walks, the ground shakes and trembles under His Holiness.

The truth is, God has a Nature about Himself as well. He is Holy, and in His Holiness, He maintains a Standard that never waives, which is far above what we could ever produce in our human being. The real mystery for us is that the more we give in our worship to Him, the more we receive. The more we seek in Him through our worship, the more we find. It's all about Worshipping God without restricting ourselves to us and our needs, and all these things shall be given unto you. Stop asking and start worshipping! The biggest heartache for the Almighty is that within His Desire for us to Worship Him, all we do is complain and suffer Him to do our bidding. The Church calls that worship, calling out to God for help. Asking and asking and asking and never completely giving of our heart, soul and mind to Him. To love the Lord your God is not just believing in Him but giving up your selfish desires and dying in them for Him! In the midst of your problems, in the midst of your personal wants and desires, stop asking and start worshiping Him, concentrate on Him like there is nothing else in your life that matters but Him. Make Him your heart's desire, make Him your mindset, make Him your First Love and Master. Love Him so much that you have no care any longer. Stop worshiping the creation (your world) and start worshiping the Creator (God).

He already knows our every need before it even occurs, before we even know about it, before we could ever ask Him for help with it. His complete Motivation with us is through Faith, Faith that has no doubt and no restriction through our Worship towards Him.

God was showing me that my transformation from sin to Salvation when I had called upon His Holy Name so many years ago, assured me a place in the Lamb's Book of the Living and my Eternal standing before Him through Eternity, but it was only the beginning of understanding His Desire for me to worship Him. Calling upon His Holy Name gave me (us) a rebirth, but in return He demands my (our) Worship (as a Believer and Follower of the Way, The Truth and The Life – Yeshua ADONAI).

When God proclaimed that He gave His Only Begotten Son, so that no one would perish, but that all could receive Eternal Life; that wasn't an act of Servitude on His part, it was the Sovereign Will of the Holy God being manifested. His fulfillment to pay the debt of our sins through the means of His Eternal Sacrifice (Yeshua HaMashiach) was His Act of Clemency towards all of humankind (Past, Present and Future).

In our fallen state (defiled sinful state of being), in which our spirit occupies this physical flesh body, we are destined to replicate repeated acts of our sinful nature, which is the natural cause of Calamity in the physical universe and in the human World Order, not to mention the outcome of Death as a result of its curse and punishment as Commanded by God. God did not Command our disobedience towards Him, even though He created the means for it to occur, His Faithful Hope in giving us a Free Will to choose the outcome of Righteousness and or Evil, was to bring Glory unto Himself, through our Faithful Attendance of acknowledging His Holiness. All things in Heaven and on earth, where Life Emanates from and is extended too, has the same Divine and Holy Purpose in its Creation, which is to Worship Him who Sits on the Throne and to bring Great Glory and Honour to His Holy Presence and unto His Holy Name.

I want to tell you what ADONAI has revealed to me about His Displeasure with the Church, the Body of Yeshua HaMashiach, which is the assemblage of the Church, not its membership, but the complete accountability of each and every person written in the Lamb's Book of the Living. It is to this accountability that God has Ordered His Salvation and Eternal Life too. The natural order that God has Commanded all of Creation is to Worship Him, and I also tell you that the Body of Yeshua ADONAI (The Church) is not Worshipping, it is a show and the Spirit Greives because of it.

I tell you, that the world gives Him no Worship, the world is dead to Him and will most definitely fall under His Righteous Judgement into Eternal Damnation. But it is the Assembly of the Church and the so-called "Houses of Worship" which are in many instances, no better than the world, in fact they fall under even greater condemnation because of the false pretense in which they bring damnation to their parishioners. Blind Guides and Serpents full of venomous poison promoting the outward appearance of what looks like a mitzvah of worship and holiness, teaming with performance and show, adorned with glamor and a show of wealth and pride, but the Church has no idea what true and faithful Worship towards God is. The kind of Worship He is wanting for and requiring in His Desire from all of His Creation.

He collectively brings all individual worship together unto Himself as the True Assembly of Believers in the Church. Our Assemblage and gathering together for whatever purposes, is not the Command in which He Desires our Worship. This is for our benefit, to gather together and have fellowship only pleases God if the outcome is to Worship Him. It is not to make a show out of the gathering together as if it is a Sunday obligation or holy assemblage of the faithful, or business club setting or to get away and isolate from the worldly order of things. Yeshua said that when two or more are gathered in My Name, I AM in the midst of them. He is being Faithful in always being there when Believers gather together for one purpose only, and that is to Worship Him. He is automatically in their midst because He is willing and waiting to Receive Worship and thus be Glorified in the Midst of the gathering together of Believers. The mere fact that some people (Christians) get together and talk about God or discuss the Bible is not the kind of Worship God is waiting to receive. Worship is not the awareness of God or the intellectual knowledge and teaching about Him; it is the individual expression of Spirit felt Love and Servitude to hunger for God without wanting or receiving any benefit in return. When Yeshua said. "*If you love me, then keep my Commandments*", was not a proclamation for us to live by the law, but the single Commandment, "to Love the Lord Your God with all of your Heart, Soul and Strength", "and to Worship no other". The whole theme of this proclamation is based on one thing and one thing only, <u>WORSHIP</u>! God demands our Worship. It is the Highest Order of our Purpose with Him. There is no other reason for our existence except to bring Him Glory through our Worshiping of Him. Our fellowship with each other is ordained by God for nothing less than our Worship of Him. Let's make it quite clear here, this is not about us or our blessing from God, or God giving us anything; this is all about God and Him receiving from us our faithful and unadulterated Worship so that He is Glorified in all that we do!

When you go "On Your Knees", we go before the Throne of God, Naked, Asking Nothing for ourselves, keeping in mind that He and He alone is God Almighty and is Totally Worthy to Receive Great Glory and Honour. We cannot bring any Burden before Him in asking for ourselves, but rather we lift up to Him our Pleasure of Praise and Honour and Worship to Him that Created All Things in Heaven and Earth and Everything within it.

The mystery in all of this for us to grasp hold of, is that Yeshua ADONAI and Elohim are One-in-the-Same, and that ABBA YAHWEH and Yeshua ADONAI are One-in-the-Same, and that Ruach HaKodesh and Yeshua ADONAI are One-in-the-Same. That there is no other Source of Holiness in Heaven or on Earth, and that all Worship is to be directed and given only to this Source and no other.

Always go before God "On Your Knees". Ask nothing, only Worship Him who has the power to kill both spirit and flesh. Fear the Lord your God and come before Him "**On Your Knees**".

15

"My Ways are not your ways"
(Written in June 2016)

To the Believers of the Way, the ones whose names are written in the Lamb's Book of the Living; from your brother Ken, who is an Elder in the Church and who has been called by the Great God and Saviour Yeshua ADONAI, to be a Teacher and Witness of what is being spoken by the Spirit so that you will be aware of your place in all of this.

Thus says the Lord God Almighty (El Shaddai), "*My Thoughts are not your thoughts, neither are your ways My Ways*" (*Isaiah 55:8*). This demonstrates a Higher Order and a much Grander Scale of Thought and Ability, especially when projecting His Sovereign Will over His Creation, in Heaven and here on Earth. His Absolute Ability to Govern all things absolutely is unquestionable. He is **Omniscient** (All-Knowing), aware of the Past, Present and Future. He is **Omnipotent** (All-Powerful), He has control over nature and has no physical limitations. He is **Omnipresent** (All-Present), He encompasses the whole universe, everywhere at the same time, there is no location that He does not inhabit. The Lord God Almighty is also **Omnibenevolent** (All-Good), He chooses to Project Goodness and reflects that through His Love and Justice. God's substance is **Holy** and because He is Holy, He is **Eternal** (No Beginning and No End).

The Lord God (ADONAI) gives us His Purpose, He is our Defender and Guardian. He honours Himself through our Faith and Rejoices when we Worship Him and show Him Respect. He is our Protector and holds us in the Palm of His Hand. The Lord God Loves the Righteous but He hates the unrighteous. He spits them out of His Mouth and brings Judgement upon them. But, as for those who faithfully love Him and whom He shows His Favour towards, He will give them a seat at His Table and in His Abode, which He has already prepared a place for them. We who love Him and are written in the Lambs Book of the Living, are called by name to be His Children and He is our Father.

The Lord God Almighty says, "*My Ways are not your ways*". In order to fulfill His Will, God gives us His Purpose. He determines what is Good and what is Evil. He commits NO Sin, for He is without any sin or condemnation that can be made of any action He takes with His Creation, in Heaven or on the Earth.

Who is like the Lord God, to Create all things in Heaven and on Earth, and to make Heaven His Abode and the Earth His Footstool.

Who is like the Lord God, who banished Adam and Eve from the Garden of God because of their Sin of Blasphemy against His Command not to partake in the fruit from the tree in the middle of the garden with the Knowledge of Good and Evil.

Who is like the Lord God, for allowing Satan to tempt the woman (Eve) and then her husband (Adam) to partake in Disobedience and Blasphemy by eating of the forbidden fruit, and pronouncing a Death Sentence upon mankind for doing it.

128

Who is like the Lord God, that placed a mark on Cain which cursed him because he murdered his brother Abel and abandoned him to the Land of NOD (Wandering).

Who is like the Lord God, who brought Abram out of the Land of UR to make His Covenant with him, and made him into the Father of many Nations (Abraham), and the Chosen People of God.

Who is like the Lord God, to pass Judgement and rain Fire and Brimstone from Heaven upon Sodom and Gomorrah and kill all of their inhabitance because of their perverted wickedness that they would not turn away from.

Who is like the Lord God, who brought plagues upon the Land of Egypt in Judgement of Moses' plea to let His People go from bondage.

Who is like the Lord God, that parted the Red Sea and save the Israelites from Pharaoh's Army. Then drowned them all for their unrighteous deeds in persecuting His People.

Who is like the Lord God, to supply Manna each day for 40 years to feed the Children of Israel while they were in the Wilderness.

Who is like the Lord God, to send us the Ten Commandments and the Law through His Servant Moses.

Who is like the Lord God, to order the Prophet Samuel, that King Saul should fight against the Amalekites and completely destroy them and everything that belongs to them. Kill every man, women, child, little babies, all the cattle and sheep and camels and donkeys... Everything. This was His Commandment.

Who is like the Lord God, to forgive King David for committing Adultery with Bathsheba and murdering her husband Uriah so he could have her for his own.

Who is like the Lord God, to show His Great Power through Elijah the Prophet against the Prophets of Baal and command that all 450 of them be brought down to the Kishon Valley where he killed them all in the presence of the Lord God.

Who is like the Lord God, to save Shadrach, Meshach and Abednego from Nebuchadnezzar's fiery furnace for not worshiping him as God. An Image of the Son of Man was in the midst of the fire with them and saved them from being burned alive; not even their clothing was scorched.

Who is like the Lord God, to send His only Begotten Son (*Yeshua*), to die for us on a cross at Calvary, and surrender Himself as a ransom for the forgiveness of our sins.

Who is like the Lord God, to raise Yeshua from the dead and therefore giving all who believe in Him the same Power to be raised on the Final Day of the Lord and share in God's Eternal Life.

Who is like the Lord God, to send mankind the Holy Spirit on the Day of Pentecost, so that His Spirit could live amongst us again. Being reconciled to God through the forgiveness of our sins through Faith in Yeshua ADONAI.

WHO IS LIKE THE LORD GOD!

In these few examples of ADONAI's Sovereign Authority, no one can judge the outcome of His Sovereign Right to do whatsoever He Wishes with His Creation, nor the outcome to His Purpose. No Judgement can be brought before Him to support the actions He has taken, for He is the Judge of Everything and All Things fall under His Holy Order and Judgement. We are but dust, sanctified by His Will and Created for His Purpose. The first Command to His Creation is, "*I AM the Lord your God, you shall have no other gods before Me*". "*You are to love the Lord your God with all your heart, with all your soul and with all your mind.*" These are not shallow requests, but rather Commandments from the Most High. These are not dictatorship edicts to rule over us, but rather Commands from a Loving God who sets the conditions in which we can share and receive Everlasting and Eternal Life with Him, and stand before Him, Holy and Righteous. Our obedience to His Sovereign Will is not a request, but rather a Commandment. Because He Loves us so much and we are so dear to His Heart,
He is a Jealous God and takes no rivals. There is nothing above Him or Beside Him; everything is below Him. He claims this to the Highest Order:

"*I AM the Lord your God, I AM ADONAI*"

16

Science (Fact or Fiction / Truth or Lie)
(Written in December 2014)

From Ken, who by Faith has been called by the Great God and Saviour, Yeshua Adonai (Jesus the Christ), to be a Believer and Teacher for the edification of the Believers of the Way, the Church or Body of Yeshua. May God the Father (ABBA YAHWEH), who has given us the Holy Spirit (Ruach HaKodesh), open your eyes and your heart to the Truth and bring you Peace according to your Faith.

This again is what the Lord has purposed me to tell you and write down so that you may be made aware in order to strengthen your Faith in the One True God, Yeshua Adonai…Amen.

Adonai wants you to be knowledgeable and that your knowledge be based in the Truth regarding what He has Created, and the substantiation of what man believes to be the truth through the evidence and physical reckoning of science. The situation for people that don't believe in God or are totally indulged into the calculating evidence of science, is that they refuse to understand and overlook the reality that God created Everything they use as physical evidence to prove and or disprove the existence of God. This of course is opposed to the Holy Essence of Elohim who is Spirit and unseen, where out of Him everything that is physical (seen) and Spirit (unseen) came from.

This is why Elohim took on physical form, in order to commune and convey with His physical creation (seen), just as He does within His Abode (Spirit-unseen). He chose to do this with the only physical beings that He had Created in His Image (embodied His Spirit), which is mankind (Human Beings), we are the Highest Order within all of His Creation.

Science is man's derivative (Macro or Microscopic) which can base the substance of inquiry and supposition related to the physical universe. Science attempts to accomplish this through Theorems, Analytical and Arithmetic Modeling, Datum, Laboratory Research and Experimental Testing, and Quorum Debate to the Supposition of Principles, which will eventually provide factual evidence for or against a standardized Thesis or quantify a Universal Law.

Science gives mankind knowledge of the obvious assumptions to his physical and seeable dimensions and manipulates the substance of physical matter. It becomes the basis to identify all truth relative to the Laws of Physics and the entire Human Experience.

Science through the best of Man's ability, can only substantiate what is part of this physical universe and the activities associated with it, which is temporal; but it cannot substantiate that which is unseen (Spirit), which is the actual Life Force and proponent of producing all which is physical (seen), which is Eternal.

It is indeed awestruck that out of all the approximately 8.3 million species on this planet (Approx. 2 million being animal types), that only Homo Sapiens (Human Beings) have the position among them as the Highest Order of Creation. We rule the planet completely.

Among the variable of species, humans are the only endothermic vertebrate mammal to walk upright which possess a brain that has two Cerebral Hemispheres that is bridged by a 6-layered neocortex, which has allowed us to think collectively and build language and exchange communication between God and man. We are the only species on earth or in the entire universe that God calls "His Children" and we call Him "Our Father".

Science relies completely on the collection of physical evidence and the extrapolation of Data in order to concede that discovery has been vindicated by conclusive findings which can be validated by the Data. Therefore, if the Data is wrong, then the evidence is tainted, and the discovery is not vindicated to a reliable conclusion. So, because both of these scenarios can exist in the Scientific Method, one called "Good Science" and the other called "Bad Science", where does Truth Prevail?

Well, the vindication of the discovery is based on the findings being agreed upon. So, in this manner, any findings can either be Truth or False, nevertheless, they will be incorporated as the "Truth" if agreed upon. The manipulation of Data is an important factor in showing the discovery has validated conclusion.

From the Human Theology, Science has no God, Science is God! The Human Intellect is only a small portion of what God has allowed man to evolve in. Humankind's evolution is not a physical transformation, but rather a Spiritual Rebirth Transformation. We are

Spirit Beings having a Human Experience, and it is temporal.

This physical Human Experience is also relative to the Physical Universe, they are interlocked and tied together, as if one in the same. Man's physical presence in the physical universe is no coincidence; and it is not just a coincidence that only mankind can explore and make discoveries about the universe and invent the science and mathematics that guide that discovery.

The logical assumption that with all of the billions of galaxies and within them are billions of stars and possible millions of planets circling those stars, is that Life as we know it must be throughout the universe, and we are not the only source of intelligent beings. The assumption is based highly around the Theory of Probability and Evolution, that throughout the universe where there is earth like planets that could possibly have liquid water, microbes living in that water could evolve into higher organisms and then into primal species and finally primates and them into higher level intelligence (human-like). Nevertheless, this theory has no empirical evidence to any fact. It is a purely speculative assumption based on a dream and misinterpretation of fossil findings from an individual who later in his life ended up disclaiming it. It was a great attempt to disclaim the Genesis story of Creation by using a so-called scientific model based on physical evidence from a long study of displaced fossil species remaining on one particular island here on earth.

God created Mankind as an extension of Himself (Elohim) in order to give witness to His Majesty and participate in His Creation and He let it come through man in order to establish the Life Presence in the entire universe. We and the earth itself are unique within the entire universe. God Himself made that declaration by saying that, Heaven was His Abode, and the Earth was His Footstool (Isaiah 66:1). This states unequivocally, that from His Presence in Heaven, He created the Earth to be the only point where He communes with Life (His Footstool) and Mankind (Humans) are the only point of that Life Communication equal to God Himself. There is no other!

The vastness of the physical universe is a mystery and the purpose of it is to demonstrate the awesomeness of God's personality with His Creation. It is a reminder to us all every time we look up into the sky that we are beholding His Majesty and Handiwork. That within the dimensional characteristic of our sight we can see His Presence. That from the unseen dimension of His Abode, He projects Himself in manner of Power, Authority and Presence.

When man acquired the Knowledge of Good and Evil, he did so in a manner that separated him from God. In the Realm of God's Perspective, which far exceeds man's limited physical and mental perspective, it's all His to begin with. He is the Creator and everything that stands before him in both Spirit's and Flesh have come out of His Eternal Being.

Even in the understanding of how the physical universe came about, man can only search for answers through his science, and the beginning of that understanding needs a starting point. There has to be some physical beginning, a pinpoint of matter which exploded into everything we can see in the physical creation. It is totally inconceivable for science to equate, that from Nothingness came the entire content of the physical universe.

The acceptable theory and axiom is that there was a beginning pinpoint of condensed substance and energy the size of a pinpoint which spanned a region of only 1×10^{-33} centimeters, and that in an undetermined instant, it exploded outward to 360 degrees with such extreme force and velocity that within $t=1\times10^{-43}$ seconds 90% of all the known mass of the universe was expelled. As if it was a little hole coming forth through a tremendous veil, bursting forth the unmeasurable force of substance and heat (in the Trillions of degrees) that what was behind it. That within 380,000 years after the initial Explosive Event, or "Big Bang", the universe had cooled enough for atoms to begin forming and quantum physics was being birth.

That behind the veil of Nothingness, where the Abode of God is, was the Eternal Substance of having No Beginning and No End. Spirit without form, Pure Energy, not cosmic but something unspeakable and beyond imaginary. Something Theologians call "Supernatural". There is no science that can explain that no hard evidence of something that you can pick apart and scrutinize. What we are witnessing is the aftermath and result of the Power that produced the Event. So, science calls it fiction, not substantiated by the known Laws of Physics or Quantum Theory. It becomes the proponent of Nay-Sayers who will use any leverage to make it seem like a fallacy rather than reality.

When you can't label something, then you mislabel it, you put it into the realm of something that only a little child with a vague understanding of reality and experience would accept...a Fairytale.

The expressed mantra and testimony of the atheist that there is no physical evidence of God's existence is absolutely false. Everything around us gives testimony to His Majesty and Existence. Where there is Absolution in the midst of a fallen world, Perfection out of Imperfection, Faith, Hope and Love prevails when Doubt abides, the burden of sin takes on the yoke of forgiveness, that through Faith denial becomes the confession of the Truth and the prevailing Science of God.

God is more real than that loaf of bread you are holding in your hand, or that brick wall you just ran into. That which is unseen is greater than that which is seen, because all things were made from that which is unseen.

Science is the exemplary attempt of man to measurably express and justify the reality of his physical existence and all facts related to that existence from beginning to end. It expressly denies anything labeled as Supernatural or Faith Based as unprovable through Scientific Methods or the Laws of Quantum Physics. But science is showing that the beginning of the physical universe came about from the opposite of what the physical universe can substantiate. There is no way to reproduce the force and mechanics that created all things as we know it through the science we have before us.

Something was behind the Vail of Nothingness that spewed forth all that we see before us. Could that something be GOD? The answer to that question is, "Most Assuredly!"

17

Was Yeshua (Jesus) Promoting the Law, or Fulfilling all Righteousness?

(Written in July 2020)

If the Judeo-Christian "Bible" reveals to us anything, it's that ELOHIM has a purpose for everything that He does, and it completely Glorifies Himself to the extent of His Satisfaction and Sanctification. In the first book of the Torah, the Genesis Story reveals that ELOHIM Created out of nothing everything in Heaven and on earth; that He Created all of the physical universe and all substance that can be seen and unseen within it. It also reveals that YAHWEH is the Creator of all Life in Heaven and on earth and throughout the physical universe that can be seen and unseen within it. It reveals that YAHWEH is the Sovereign Lord (ADONAI) over all these things and He has Supreme Power and Authority and is Eternal in His Being; and within His Nature His Judgement is Righteous and Everlasting.

In the Judeo-Christian "Bible", the Fourth Testimony of the New Covenant that ELOHIM made with mankind, which is the Gospel according to John the Apostle of Yeshua HaMashiach (Jesus the Messiah), reveals that

ELOHIM Created Everything that was ever Created in Heaven and on earth and throughout the physical universe that can be seen and unseen through His "Word", The Word of YAHWEH; and that the Word became a man (Flesh) and lived among us and revealed His Glory, the Glory of the Father. That the "Word" was in fact the Son of God, the Only Begotten, Full of Grace, to whom the Propitiation of Sin would be given through; and that through His Death and Resurrection Salvation would be afforded to all mankind.

That during His Visitation on earth, He revealed Himself to the physical creation and all of the physical universe as the Son of God and as being One with the Father, The HaMashiach (Messiah) and King of Israel, and the Saviour of the World (All Mankind); and stipulated the conditions in which mankind would be forgiven of their Captivity to Sin (Complete Clemency) and thereby have afforded Salvation through Him and the Gift of Everlasting and Eternal Life.

The Extenuating Purpose of His Visitation was to manifest the fulfillment of all Righteousness through the

Law (Torah); and subdue the Law and the Religion perpetuated through it, by means of fulfilling that which was written by the Prophets and was referenced by Moses as the fulfillment of all Righteousness through the coming of HaMashiach (Messiah) and King.

Why would this manifestation be anticipated? That for His Namesake, YAHWEH would rescue mankind and bring about the Forgiveness of all their sins through the act of Propitiation, thereby casting them from Himself as far away as the East is from the West and would remember them No More! Under the Law, YAHWEH made a Provision (a way out) through an Atonement (Covering Over) of Sin for the Nation, which occurred once a year (Yom Kippur). Under the Law, the High Priest would give a Blood Sacrifice and Burnt Offering in order to reconcile the accumulated sins of the Children of Israel (the Entire Nation) before ADONAI, and ELOHIM would Credit their sins for another year; with the acknowledgement that eventually, this Credit would have to be Paid in Full. This is where HaMashiach (Messiah) and King would come, and He would then take the Atonement Credit and through His Propitiation, pay it in Full and the account for Sin would be Closed Forever and would accumulate No More!

Now, in order to fulfill the Righteous and Eternal Conditions of Forgiveness and the Propitiation of all the sins of mankind (past, present and future); ELOHIM Himself would have to Proclaim and Fulfill these conditions and thus, satisfy all Righteousness in accordance to His Standard as He proclaimed them within the Law and then bring about the Salvation of all mankind under a New Order and New Covenant which would be sustained by Faith and not be subject to the Law any longer.

The New Kingdom and Covenant would be fulfilled by the birth of the HaMashiach (Messiah) and King in accordance with the Prophetic Scriptures as highlighted:
- HaMashiach will come from the Line of Abraham (Genesis 12:3)
- HaMashiach will be born of a virgin (Isaiah 7:4)
- HaMashiach will be a descendent of Isaac and Jacob (Genesis 17:19)
- HaMashiach will be born in the town of Bethlehem, Israel (Micah 5:2)
- HaMashiach will be called out of Egypt (Hosea 11:1)

- HaMashiach will be from the Tribe of Judah (Genesis 49:10)
- HaMashiach will enter the Temple (Malachi 3:1) Note: This is important because the Temple was destroyed by the Romans in 70AD and never rebuilt.
- HaMashiach will be from the lineage of King David (Jeremiah 23:5)
- Mashiach's birth will be accompanied by great suffering and sorrow (Jeremiah 31:15)
- HaMashiach will fulfill all Righteousness, die by crucifixion, be resurrected from death, ascend into Heaven and sit at the Right Hand of God (Psalm 22:16, Psalm 16:10, Zechariah 13:7, Isaiah 53:10-11, Psalm 68:18, Psalm 110:1)

In all of our humanity and history, there has been no one person who has fulfilled all of the conditions of Prophecy and Righteousness to be identified as the HaMashiach (Messiah) and King, other than the man, Yeshua of Nazareth. Many false prophets have called themselves Messiah and Christ but could not and have not fulfilled the required conditions to be HaMashiach and King. Only one man has been able to completely fulfill and exceed the Prophetic Conditions and

Requirements of the HaMashiach and King of Israel; and that is Yeshua of Nazareth (the Man God). It was by His Death and Blood Sacrifice that the Conditions for the Complete and Utter Forgiveness of Sins could be made and Satisfy the Debit of Atonement, by which Propitiation of Sins could be wiped out from the Mind and Sight of ELOHIM Forever. It was also afterwards, by His Resurrection from Death, that He made the Way for all mankind to receive Everlasting and Eternal Salvation through a heartfelt Belief and Confession from any person to recognize that He (Yeshua HaMashiach) is ADONAI and ELOHIM; and that they (the Confessor) would receive this Salvation through Yeshua (Jesus the Christ) by Faith (which has No Doubt) and not by any condition of the Law or that of Works.

For the Church, the Law is no longer validated, but rather Faith is Supreme to fulfill all Righteousness.
Faith in Yeshua HaMashiach! (Matthew 28:18-20, John 1:1-4, John 3:16-17, John 14:6-7, 1John 5:19-20, Romans 3:10,22-23, Romans 10:9-13, Romans 14:11, Ephesians 2:4-9, 2Timothy 1:9, Titus 3:4-7, Revelation 20:11-15)

18

Good Friday? or should it be Good Thursday
(Written in November 2020)

My Dearest Brethren, from Ken who is an Elder and Teacher in the Church of Yeshua ADONAI. I was a practicing Jew at one time, but found my way to the Truth, the Way and the Life through a personal conviction and revelation from ADONAI Himself. I pray that in your reading of this letter; you find awareness to what God the Father (ABBA YAHWEH) is revealing to the Church of the Way and to correct any misconception about what dogmatic tradition and truth really are.

The cornerstone of God's Forgiveness and the Propitiation of all Sin, as well as His Gift to us of Salvation and Everlasting Life, is the Gospel of Yeshua ADONAI. Tradition and Religious Order are the worst enemy of the Truth and have imposed false and inaccurate doctrine to be ordained within our Christian Fellowship and Assembly. By order and decree of Church Dogma from many different religions throughout the centuries and millennium, and through mis-transliterations of the original Gospel text and language, many of the actual dates, events and translation of phrases and words that Yeshua was expounding are inaccurate and wrongfully understood.

Since after the Apostolic Age when the Apostles died away and Dogma began to divide the Christian Church into Religious Orders, the original passing of the Truth by mouth regarding" The Way" (Gospel of Yeshua) became broken. It became written as Testimonies and Eye-Witnessed accounts from various sources which were hard to collaborate. This is why Fables engulf the Bible between the Old and New Testaments. This is why peoples and Sects divide into Religious Denominations and fight among themselves to be recognized as the true Christian Order. The Heathen Nations and peoples (Gentiles) are coming into the "Born Again" Church experience and Christianity as a religious order from many different cultural and life-style perspectives (being raised outside of Judaism) and are totally misguided in understanding the culture of the Bible from its original lifestyle and historic perspective. The format and protocols for converting Gentiles into Christians are not being taught the proper context of the nature in which God is purposing His Creation and the interaction He is working through it. It is being taught from a Renewed Gentile perspective, as a Christian in the cultural setting of modern times and not from a Hebrew perspective in which it was written and lived in those times. Christians are not being taught about the Jewish Jesus (Yeshua), only the Saviour Jesus, but in order to properly understand how and why Yeshua became our Saviour, we must first understand the full context and perspective of Him being a Jew and why He had to be both Prophet and Redeemer of the Law and Fulfil all Righteousness under the Law in order to free us from it and in doing so in a Jewish way (God's Hebrew Perspective), in order to free us (Jews and Gentiles) from all Sin and open the door to Everlasting and Eternal Life. The Forgiveness and Salvation of all Mankind came about because Yeshua, during His visitation, Fulfilled the entire Law, and in particular The Law of Atonement.

It is absolutely imperative that what we are reading in the translated Bibles and being taught by our Church Leadership (Pastors, Evangelists, Teachers, etc.) out of Seminary are the actual words and terms which were used in the original Hebrew, Greek and Aramaic text, so that the language in which we are transliterating them into is exactly what was being said; and most importantly, that the expressions of the phrasing of these words are interpreted properly in accordance with the way they were being used at the time and generation they were being spoken from. We must also be in-tune to the dialect and synonyms involved from the writer's language and cultural perspective, we cannot always interpret what the Gospels or any referenced biblical writings have to say at face value to our current language and dialect, especially the English Language.

One such mistranslated event of extreme importance, is the Good Friday Scenario, which has been accepted through tradition as the day in which Yeshua was Executed (Crucified) prior to the Shabbat Passover. This has been wrongfully accepted and misguided by Church Dogma, tradition, and mis-transliteration. Part of this is due to the Interpreters lack of knowing the common language and associated terms commonly used with the dialect of that time; and the chronological events in association with the actual Jewish Passover Festival and Special Shabbat that was occurring in this year's Passover cycle. It's not that the writer was wrong in how they wrote down the events taking place, but rather, the translation of Hebrew Aramaic and Greek was misinterpreted in the transliteration between languages as well as the cultural dialect being used in phrasing at the time.

It is important to be knowledgeable of the fact that the Gospel according to Matthew was written entirely in Hebrew, where the other Gospels according to Mark, Luke and John were written in Greek. Matthew gives the accurate chronological account of the Crucifixion leading from the week prior to the two festivals in which the first is where Yeshua held the Passover Meal (Last Supper), on Wednesday sundown and the evening before and after, leading into the Special Shabbat (Festival of Unleavened Bread), which began on Thursday sundown and lasted through Friday, then the Weekly Shabbat which began on Friday sundown.

The Gospel of John, however, gives the beginning day to Matthews chronological timeline of the events. In John 12:1, he states, "Six days before the Passover, Yeshua came to Bethany, where Lazarus lived, whom Yeshua had raised from the dead." This was the Saturday before the Passover. Then in John 12:12-15 it states, "The next day the great crowd that had come for the festival heard that Yeshua was on his way to Jerusalem. They took palm branches and went out to meet him, shouting, "Hoshana!" "Blessed is he who comes in the name of the Lord!" "Blessed is the King of Israel!" Yeshua found a young donkey and sat on it, as it is written: "Do not be afraid, Daughter Zion; see, your King is Coming, seated on a donkey's colt." This was Sunday, or what is considered to be Palm Sunday (Day 2), which meant that four (4) days hence would be Thursday.

According to the Gospel accounts, Yeshua was arrested after the Passover Meal sometime in the late evening on Wednesday, and brought before the Sanhedrin for trial and pronounced guilty of blasphemy for claiming to be the Son of God (Equal to God), then routed to Pilate for questioning about sedition and a declaration of disturbing the peace of the Empire, then routed to King Herod sometime in the early morning (AM) Thursday before sunrise, for questioning of His claim of blasphemy, then back to Pilate again to address the crime of sedition (claiming to be the King of the Jews), where He was assaulted, brutally beaten and flogged after sunrise, then sentenced to death by Pilate for the crime of sedition. He was forced to carry His own Crucifixion Cross through the streets of Jerusalem to the outer city, a place called the Skull-Golgotha (Calvary), and was nailed to the Cross, then upright erected and suffered Crucifixion from 9am until 3pm Thursday afternoon, when He cried out "It is Finished", then gave up His Spirit and died. He had to be taken down from the Cross and placed in burial before sundown on Thursday because of the start of the Special Shabbat (Festival of Unleavened Bread), which followed the Passover that year.

Now, for you non-Jewish people, which is about 99% of all Born Again Christians in the United States, the Meal associated to the Festival of Unleavened Bread was called the Seder. In modern times, after the destruction of the Holy Temple in Jerusalem (70AD), the Seder started being associated with the Passover Meal (continuing in these modern times today), because of the disruption of all the Rituals and Festivals according to the Law of Moses not being fulfilled any longer without the Temple in Jerusalem. It was this Festival and Meal which has been mistranslated into the English Bible account of this Passover Meal (Last Supper), one day later (after) the Passover of that year was actually held. This means that the traditional Crucifixion Day of Yeshua (Friday) was actually Thursday in conjunction to the Passover of that year, and not Friday which would have put it a day later into the Shabbat of the Festival of Unleavened Bread (Seder), and then rolling right into the Weekly Shabbat (back-to-back Shabbats).

It's not that the Gospel account is wrong, but the transliteration of language and script translation is inaccurate with certain aspects of the Gospel accounts; it's like that throughout many areas of the English Bible. But it is critical that the account to its proper chronology is accurate, because of the prophecy that Yeshua had given about His resurrection occurring in three days and three nights, according to the Miracle of Jonah (Matthew 12:40). Scholars have been at odds in trying to justify the Gospels timeline for the three days and three nights that Yeshua was supposed to be in the grave before He rose from the dead (as the prophecy that Yeshua had predicted). I mean, how do you get three days and evenings from late afternoon on Friday to sunrise on Sunday. Well, the answer is,

<u>"YOU DON'T"</u>.

Historical fact and Biblical account do not match, and the reason is, Church tradition and dogma do not want to give way to mis-transliteration and translation in order to give a proper account, which exceeds what is considered the unwavering authority of every word within the Bible as being "The Infallible Word of God". The label of "Holy Bible" seals that perception and aggregates preponderance of its fact to the world-wide consortium of the "Holy Church" and places it above ALL other religious truths and revelation. Anything other than it being considered as "Infallible" would mean that it comes from man rather than God; and

thus, could not emphatically be used to rule over Empirical Church Doctrine and Evangelical Teaching, and could not be claimed by the masses of Seminary Institutions as the "Word of God". Notwithstanding, this would be considered to invalidate any Ordained Appointment of Pastoral Decree and remove the "Holy Order" of the Christian Church.

The Bible is the written account and references (Testimony) to the identity and workings of the Holy God and His relationship with His Creation. It was written by men and most definitely inspired by God, The Holy Spirit (Ruach HaKodesh). It speaks of many truths and relates references to many accounts (stories) of the outcome between God's Purpose with mankind in their fallen state (sin) and how He (God) will bring Man back to a perfect and redemptive state with Him. But, more than anything, it tells us and speaks to the "Word of God", who and what that is.

All through the Bible, it leads up to and finally identifies who the "Word of God" is. It is not the words within the Bible (the Written Word), but rather, the Living Word (Yeshua ADONAI) the Son of the Living God (John 1:1-14). This is the Infallible Word of God and is Life Eternal! (1John 5:19)

Brethren, we need to be mindful that Christianity has its beginnings and is rooted in the Jewish Faith with all of its Laws, Festivals and Traditions, which
Yeshua of Nazareth was upholding and expounding upon in both His Rabbinical and Prophetic quest to fulfil all Righteousness as the Son of God.

What the Old Testament (Tanakh) identified and promised through prophecy regarding the Messiah and His Coming, was fulfilled through the witness and testimony of Yeshua of Nazareth during His Visitation on earth. He was establishing and bringing forth the Kingdom of God and pronouncing that our "Captivity from Sin" was over. His Purpose was not going to coincide with the traditional Jewish understanding of what Messiah was going to achieve, in that He would be proclaimed as the King of Israel and restore the Throne of David; and thus, defeat all of His enemies and establish His Earthly Kingdom and rule from Jerusalem forever.

Under no condition of either misinformation, teaching or ignorance, should any of us in the Body of ADONAI not understand the true meaning of the Lord God's Visitation through Yeshua of Nazareth 2000 years ago. In fulfillment of all the writings of the Prophets, of Moses and the Psalms, the appointed time had come for God to reveal Himself to His People (Israel) as their Messiah

(HaMashiach), and to fulfill the Fathers Will to the Children, of releasing their Captivity from Sin and Renew what Adam had separated by his disobedience and blasphemy in the Garden of God. God was now, at this time in our human history, bringing all of His human creation back to where they were in the Garden of God before Adam became sin. He (Yeshua) came as the Incarnate God, as the Son of God, to replace what Adam had destroyed and fulfill all Righteousness under the Law of Moses and become the Final Atonement - Lamb of God, to be sacrificed for all of mankind and take upon Himself all of the Sins of the Atonement through the Law and give complete Propitiation through His Death to all mankind and establish a permanent way for Salvation through being the First Born (Son of God) Resurrected from the Dead.

It must also be understood that God never intended (Purposed) for man to be separated from Himself as a Living Being. Once the Lord God breathed the Spirit of Life (Holy Spirit) into Adam, he became a Living Being and the gateway to Eternal Life had been established between God and His Creation in this universe here on earth.

Out of all the preparation that Yeshua did during His Earthly Ministry to reveal and demonstrate to Israel that He was indeed the Messiah, the Son of God, the final and most important event was His Crucifixion and Resurrection Three Days later. This was to be Three Full days and Three Full Evenings in order for the Prophecy of the Miracle of Jonah that Yeshua Prophesied to be fulfilled (Matthew 12:39-42). During

the infancy of the Church after the 1st Century AD, the Bible was being establish
with the Hebrew Bible including the Old Testament (Tanakh) and the New Testament (HaBrit HaChasasha) being completed sometime in the 2nd Century AD. The Canon of the Council of Rome was establish and conveyed at the end of the 3rd Century AD, with Canon Law being established in order to form the Rules and Order of a future Orthodox Religion; and to establish the manner in which the Dogma related to the Gospel should be defined and expounded to the Universal (Catholic) Church through the Masses.

The control and execution of this would be through the Catholic Priesthood and ordained by what the Catholic Order would pronounce as their "God on Earth" Representative, the Pope, who would become the unholy extension of ADONAI (Christ) from Heaven and execute power from the Vatican as the Ruler of the World. They (Catholics) consider themselves to be the only true Christian Order of Religion in the entire world by sanctity through the Priestly Order of the Apostle Peter, whom they claim endowed by holy proclamation as the First Pope of Rome. This means that the Pope, along with the Priestly Order would have divine intervention between God and Man; and the Pope to be the physical evidence of God in both Power and in Word, to the extension of being identified as "the Holy Father". This of course is utter blasphemy, considering Yeshua said that you are to call no man on earth Father, except God Himself (Matthew 23:9). He was referencing to the titles that men gave themselves in order for prestige and honour. However, the word

"Father" here would be an offset of the Hebrew word *HaElohim*, meaning God in His Three-Fold manner (Father, Son and Holy Spirit). So, Yeshua was pointing to Himself as the extension of the Godhead with this reference, and warning against that title being used by any man.

Even though the books of the Canon of the New Testament were written before the release of the Hebrew Bible, it is viewed that the four Gospels which were chosen to represent that Canon were finally assembled and available to the Church between the 4th and 5th Century AD. The first three Gospels (Matthew, Mark and Luke) are called the "synoptics", from a Greek phrase meaning "seen together", because they put the events of Yeshua's life in the same order and have many of the same stories and sayings, often in the same or very similar words. The fourth Gospel (The Gospel according to the Apostle John) is set aside as being different from the synoptics and even classified as anonymous. Unlike the first three Gospels, John relates that Yeshua is the Word of God and shows His Complete Divinity and Deity as God. It also relates a different timeline and reference to the Passover Shabbat and the Last Supper (John 13:1 and 19:31), and even before that time, the Apostles, and early Church Fathers (who were Jewish), lived and witnessed the times of these events and the manner in which they were written down reflected it in respect to their religious traditions and laws.

Up until the Protestant Reformation and Separatist Movement from the Roman Catholic Church was initiated by Martin Luther and continued by John Calvin, Huldrych Zwingli, and other early Protestant Reformers in 16th century Europe, Canon Law had imposed brutal punishment to anyone who opposed it. No one read anything, the Bible was not available to the Masses and not even too many of the officials within the Roman Catholic Church, only the Priesthood and the Church Hierarchy above it could interpret and expound upon the Written Word of God (through Canon Law) to the Masses. This is a practice that is still carried on to this day.

Therefore, we must be mindful, that with our walk in Yeshua, we are bold in proclaiming the Truth and set on righteousness towards seeking what the "Truth" is. The Truth is, that evil will not stand in the Presence of God except through Judgement and then Eternal Damnation. The Truth is, that ALL Righteousness is found in Yeshua ADONAI, who is the Judge of All mankind and the Redeemer of All mankind, and that no one goes to the Holy Father (ABBA YAHWEH) God the Father) except by Way of Him (Yeshua). Amen!

19

My Christmas Message
(Written in December 2021)

From a Believer in the One True God, Yeshua ADONAI, The Spirit of God is once again conveying His Displeasure with all of the inhabitance of this planet, especially the "Body of Yeshua" (The Church). God is not pleased with the behavior of The Human Race, His Highest Order of Creation, and the Heirs to His Salvation. The Word still stands in jeopardy and condemnation by saying, "Not one is righteous!" That, everything we do is as "Filthy Rags" to Him. Yet in all of this, God the Father (**Yahweh**) has given us all a way out, by first giving Propitiation of our Sins and providing us with His Everlasting Salvation through the Death and Resurrection to Life of His Son (Himself-Elohim) making anyone who will receive the Son of God (Yeshua) to become Heirs to His Kingdom and a Righteous Standing in His Sight.

The meaning behind what **Yahweh** was doing in the physical birth of the Son of God (Yeshua ADONAI) and the foregoing proclamation and announcement by Angels was not to men for good tidings; but rather was the announcement to the fulfillment of God's Prophetic Word to Redeem all Mankind back unto Himself and end our captivity to the one thing that separated the first man (Adam) from God and his seed thereafter...SIN! The second and Most Important announcement to all of mankind was in the physical manifestation and fulfillment of the Law of Atonement so that our Sins would no longer be a credit accountable to God, but the

Propitiation (clearing of that debt by God) and payment in Full forever as an Everlasting Covenant between God and Mankind. Therefore, the Son of God became the Everlasting Covenant as symbolized as the Lamb of God, the sacrifice given for the Atonement of Sin Forever. The Law now being fulfilled, the act was no longer needed to be performed. The One True Expression of God's Unconditional Love for us is in the fulfillment of the Lamb of God to be the slaughtered Passover Sacrifice whose Death and subsequent Resurrection back to Life is the Final Act to Redeem Mankind and give any of us who rest in His Redemption to share Everlasting Life and a place with Him in His Kingdom Forever. Therefore, Yeshua is the Complete Point of Worship, from Everlasting to Everlasting. He has No Beginning and No End and for us to concentrate on one or the other, leaves us open to a false intent and a false witness. We are to celebrate the One True God in our Faith and Worship continuously, not through any point of Calendar Event or Holiday, which gives precedence to those events as being higher recognition than our Daily and Momentary Worship.

As the celebration of Christmas once again motivates the world into the sale of all kinds of goods and products in the form of Gifts, the focus is towards the commercialization of the event on December 25th and reaching even higher profit margins than from the previous year (the Moneychangers of our time) and putting more people in debt than ever before. The Baby Jesus and the Holy Family are once again put on display as a show of the Christian Religious Icons which reminds us of how special this time of the year and this event really is from a commercial perspective. In fact, the reminder and celebration begin earlier and earlier each passing year. The marketing aspects used to begin right after Thanksgiving, in the infamous "Black Friday" fiasco, but as the world and even Christendom itself become more and more secular this "Cash Cow" is being displayed right after all the Labour Day sales events; and as a first, this year, in some places here in the United States it started right after the 4th of July.

More money is collected, and donations made than any other time or occasion of the year, and the Churches and religious organizations all look forward to the Faithful bringing in the last vestiges of required tithings in order to meet their total annual financial quotas. Like any other business or corporation, the Churches need their money, and besides Easter being the only other major event in the Christian celebration which packs the House and has the ability to fill the coffers, Christmas is the Motherlode. But we must not lose the perspective on who and what is the focus of this celebration.

The reason Christmas has such a great marketing effect on the entire world, especially the Christian Sect Religions, is the focus on the Divine (God), but this of course has become perverted as the world has made it into "One in the Same", and the Christians have "Bought" into the idea that Giving somehow is the same as worship towards God. Like going to church every Sunday, this kind of Celebratory Giving makes you feel good, like it's an extension of your own family, like you are performing a function that is Godly and Holy. It releases a mandate according to the Law to at least once or twice a week give some tithing and worship towards the Thing you call Holy. You claim it strengthens your Faith and brings into perspective what God wants us to do in Fellowship; again, the reality that it is a mandate fulfilling an obligation towards the Law.

Where did all the idea of Gift Giving come from to begin with. It all started Pre-Roman Days, when the Greeks gave homage to their gods for everything from good crops to good luck and having many children. The Hebrews had set days of the year in which they gave Tithings and Offerings to their God according to the Mitzvah's that God ordered. No gifts were given individually because it was seen as an offering of idolatry, only offering and Tithings were given to God through the Tabernacle (in the Wilderness) or The Temple in Jerusalem. Our current practices of giving Presents and Gifts to each other come from long standing heathen traditions, mostly Roman in nature and thus in Christianity came through the Catholic Church doctrine. Seen as a fable set around the Gifts that were given to Jesus by the Magus (Magi or Wise Men from the East), the tradition of the Masses of the Faithful giving Gifts to each other reconciled that act as Holy. But, as anything created by men and tradition, it soon became corrupt and perverted towards the Holy Relic it was supposedly paring.

The Modern Church (Laodicea) has such a membership of Perverts and Heathenistic following, because as Yeshua ADONAI spoke about these Times (The Last Days of the End-Times), people are Doers of Evil and Haters of God. They worship the identity of

God (Superficial-All Show), but not the True Form of God (Spirit).

The Birth of Yeshua ADONAI was never meant to be a Celebration, nor be made into a heathen ritual as it has been exploited by the Church and the World and especially as we express it in these Last Days of the End-Times. The Almighty is not a baby in a manger or a child that needs to be protected by his parents or schooled by any fashion of earthly proportions. He Was, Is and Will Always Be the King of Kings and the Lord of Lords. The only ones who saw that Truth were the Wise Men from the East when they gave the Prophetic Gifts of Honour, Praise and Glory to the only King and God that had appeared before them on Earth (Then, Now and Forever). The whole purpose of Yeshua being Born and living as a Human was to appease Yahweh's Atonement of our Sin and to fulfil the entire purpose and Righteousness of the Law of Moses in order to bring an end to our Captivity under the Law and of Sin.

Righteousness prevails not because of His birth, but because of His Sacrifice to do what no man could do, which was to take away the Sins of the World and Give us Everlasting Life. The celebration is that Elohim stepped down from Heaven (The Holy Place) and rendered Himself a ransom for His Highest Order of Creation in order that we may receive Salvation from the Death of Sin and Live Forever in the abode of God and share in His Kingdom forever and not be condemned to damnation as the Law orders us to be. We have been Saved by Grace, and that is the Real Celebration!

20

The Healing of the Man with Leprosy
(Written in October 2019)

I don't think a lot of people understood the significance of **Luke 5:12-14:** (*From the Hebrew perspective*)

This verse of scripture is overlooked in its importance as to the beginning Ministry of Yeshua ADONAI (Jesus the Christ). This miracle was performed at the beginning of His Ministry on Earth right after He began assembling his disciples together. It is important to note that this disease (Leprosy) was considered under the Law of Moses as being a divine judgement against an individual (Leviticus 13:1-46). In all the history of Israel, up until the moment of this miracle, no one had ever been cured of leprosy. The significance of this man that Yeshua was about to heal, is that his leprosy was (all through him), meaning that the bacterial disease had gone throughout every organ of his body and he was near death. When he came to Yeshua, it was his last effort and desperate attempt in humility when he said " **"Lord, if You are willing, You can make me clean."** The next thing that Yeshua said is the most significant, *"I am willing; be cleansed."* And then he touched the man and immediately the leprosy left him. So, why is this so significant, this miracle?

1. The Levitical Priesthood had been exercising this Law (Leviticus 13) since the time it was given by Moses. It was understood that this particular disease was so defiled that it was a divine judgement from God and incurable by human means, thus viewed as a passage of judgement imposed by God Himself and could not be revoked by man.

2. Any individual that had been declared unclean by the Priest under The Law according to Leviticus 13 was a complete and utter outcast and considered no longer a part of the community of Israel. This meant that they were not to approach or come near anyone for the rest of their life. The Law also stated that no one in Israel was to touch a Leper or they would become defiled and unclean themselves.

3. This event in Luke 5 was to fulfill a single purpose, which was to identify The Messiah in fulfillment of Isaiah 35:6. Not only did the Leper disregard The Law by approaching Yeshua, but Yeshua as an Israelite also disregarded The Law by touching him. Had Yeshua not cured this man; his identity would have not been revealed.

4. After the healing, Yeshua sternly directed the man *"But go and show yourself to the priest, and make an offering for your cleansing, as a testimony to them, just as Moses Commanded."* The significance of this was to fulfill the prophecy of Isaiah 35:6. This would be the first time that the Levitical Priesthood would have to impose The Law according to Leviticus 14, so they were utterly stunned when this man approached them to fulfill this, Law. It meant 2 things to them; 1: a miracle had been given which had never occurred before and 2: the possibility of Messiah being on the Earth was now evident.

5. The following verse of scripture in Luke 5:17 is typically overlooked by the Christian reader as a mere passage of information with no significant value.

Luke 5:17 says: "*Now it happened on a certain day, as He "(Yeshua) was teaching, that there were Pharisees and Teachers of the Law sitting by, who had come out of **every** town of Galilee, and Judea, and Jerusalem, and the power of the Lord was **present** to heal them.*" The significance of this verse of scripture can be overlooked because of the way the English translation is written by chapter & verse number. The original Greek text is not written in this manner. There are no spaces or verses, just continuous thought in the writing. So, this indicates a continuous commentary from the previous verse regarding the healing of the man and the day when Yeshua was teaching. The question which should be asked in the mind of the reader is why would Pharisees and Teachers of The Law come to where Yeshua was in Galilee, literally a hundred or more miles away, from every town in Galilee and Judea and from Jerusalem? This means there were hundreds of these people showing up in this small town where Yeshua was teaching and healing. The answer refers back to Leviticus 14 having to be imposed for the first time. They were there to witness The Messiah coming to Earth. The significance of this is in Luke 5:17 when it says, "*And the power of the Lord was present to heal them.*"

6. The witnessing of Yeshua healing an individual of something that could not be done by human means showed the Divine intervention of God which could only be performed by God, firstly in the forgiveness of sin and then the reversal of the Divine Judgement against the individual.

7. This act of forgiveness and healing together would sanctify the next miracle in Luke 5:18-26, where Yeshua healed a lame man by first forgiving his sins and then commanding him to get up and walk. The Teachers of The Law and Pharisees began to rebuke Him and claimed blasphemy because only God could forgive sins. By showing His divine personage as The Son of Man through the previous miracle, He now rebukes them by saying, "*Which is easier to say, your sins are forgiven you or get up and walk?*". Immediately the man rose to his feet, took his bed he was laying on and went home praising God.

This clearly showed that the Messiah was now on the earth and that He was in the form of a human man and that this man was Yeshua of Nazareth, whom many had already sot out as being the Messiah; but this also posed a great threat to the Teachers of the Law and the Pharisees because this would take away their focus of authority from the people and move it to this man who now was being called, "The Son of God", no one less than, the Messiah, the Second Part of the Godhead (Elohim).

[Commentary]

The one thing that has always baffled me is when Yeshua was standing before the High Priest-Caiaphas, at the convening of the Sanhedrin Trial (The Council of Elders and Rabbi's) (John 18:19-24, Matthew 26:57-68), in order to discredit Him and proclaim that He was committing blasphemy because He was being claimed as the Son of God and Messiah. The trial was a Mock Trial and totally against the ordinances of the Jewish

Law in the way it was being conducted. It was done at night (which was forbidden by the Law) and before a select few from the Sanhedrin in order to sway a guilty plea and there was no trial to convict the accused. But, even so, when they were asking for proof to the claims of Him being the Messiah (*HaMashiach*), why wasn't the Miracle of the healing of the Leprosy brought up. This was known by all of them in this trial. Everyone in the Sanhedrin already knew of it including the High Priest. The man healed was commanded by Yeshua to go and show himself before the Priest and make an Offering of Cleansing according to Leviticus 14. This was a first in all of the History of the Jews and this news spread like Wildfire throughout Israel and every sector of the Religious Communities. Members of the Sanhedrin were part of the hundreds of Religious Leaders (Pharisees and Teachers of the Law) sitting by who had come out of every town of Galilee, and Judea, and Jerusalem to witness the Presence of God in this Man Yeshua, and the Power of God was in Him to Heal them all.

This alone, according to the Law of Moses and the Prophets was unwavering proof, that Yeshua (*HaMashiach) was* the Messiah and as claimed the Son of God, and that His Deity of being One with the Father (Elohim) was secure and the undeniable Truth. Why was this not even brought up or mentioned in the Trial before the Sanhedrin or before King Herod when he was questioning Him (Luke 23:6-12). They kept asking him the question, "Are you the Son of God?', which if given to anyone else to answer Yes to, would have been utter blasphemy; but giving such a question to the

One who performed this particular miracle according to the Law of Moses, should have been them say, "You are the Son of God and Messiah!"

What this shows is two-fold: 1) The deception and evil from the Powers of Darkness to overcome the Truth even when displayed openly and without any doubt as it being the Truth can subvert men who have evil in their hearts and want only their will and desires to be kept in place. The power and authority they desire is only of man and not of God. 2) It also shows that God's Will be done, and that the Truth will stand forever before all men and before the Judgement Seat of God, who is the One whom they lied about and the One who they will stand before in the Final Day of Judgement. The ones whose names have been withheld from the Book of the Living, **The Book of Life**, and will be cast into utter darkness.

"Then I saw a great white throne and Him who sat on it, from whose face the earth and the heaven fled away. And there was found no place for them. And I saw the dead, small and great, standing before God, and books were opened. And another book was opened, which is the **Book of Life**. *And the dead were judged according to their works, by the things which were written in the books. The sea gave up the dead who were in it, and Death and Hades delivered up the dead who were in them. And they were judged, each one according to his works. Then Death and Hades were cast into the Lake of Fire. This is the second death. "And anyone not found written in the* **Book of Life** *was cast into the Lake of Fire."* (Revelation 20:11-15)

It must be remembered that this is not Kenna Outreach proclaiming this Judgement or anyone in the Body of Yeshua (Body of Christ) or the Church; this is the Written and Proclaimed Voice of God who spoke this, the Word of God! It was written down as dictated by His Apostle John and sanctified as the

Truth through the Testimony given by Yeshua Himself. "*I, Yeshua, have sent My angel to testify to you these things in the churches. I am the Root and the Offspring of David, the Bright and Morning Star.*" (Revelation 22:16)

21

Does God Love the Angels?
(Written in February 2021)

From Ken, who is an Elder in the Church and by Faith proclaims this message to be one of truth and acknowledgement from the Spirit of ADONAI and is revealed as such for His Purpose.

Does God Love the Angels is not an easy question to answer or understand from the human perspective because of the way we view what love is and how we obtain affirmation of it. Love for us is both emotional and physical. It is an expression of our highest admiration towards something or somebody. But, under undetermined circumstances we can retract our love and exchange it for remorse and regret for ever sharing it with something or someone. So, human love has conditions associated with it and those conditions vary from person to person.

God on the other hand, has no Conditions associated with His Love (*Unconditional Love*). But what is this Love that ADONAI speaks of and has commanded us towards. It is a Godly expression of fortitude and incorruptible dedication towards Himself.

The Essence of God is Spirit, for God is Spirit, but He is also Love, and from the Divine Sense these two attributes define His Holiness and are Holy in and of themselves for they are Eternal. God is Holy because He is Spirit and Eternal, with no beginning and no end. Yet the Love of God is an extension of His Eternal Love and Holiness and joins together that which He has Created.

Even so, the Love of God is not part of His Creation, it is not Human nor Angelic, it is not cosmic or metaphysical, and it is most definitely not a feeling or an emotional expression. The Love of God is His Spirit and His Eternal Glory and Essence, that which is shared with no one else. All Things came about because of the Love of God and through The Word of God (Yeshua ADONAI)

When God Created Heaven and the Abode in which He would reside His Power to go forth into Eternity, He first Created out of Spirit and Light Angelic Beings, billions and billions of pure Sources of Light dazzling and dancing like radiant shafts to the Thunderous Sound coming from the Throne of the Almighty. Then, like butterfly's coming out from their cocoons bursting forth in Servitude and in complete unisons, bellowing out deafening Praises and Honour to the Esteemed Glory of God, yelling "Holy, Holy, Holy is the Lord God Almighty", and what sounded like "Hallelujah" in the background, long a sustaining, never ending, even to this very moment. These are Creatures that were Created as Servants to perform a multitude of Commanding and Inherent tasks, fulfilling God's Divine Purpose for Him and for us (Human Beings). All of them fervently worship God and instruct and help humans,

So, they (Angelic Beings) exist in the Eternal Love of God, but do not share in His Unconditional Love that He expressly shares with His Highest Order of Creation which is mankind (Humans). It's hard to imagine any distinction between what God shows to the sum of His Creation (in Heaven and on Earth), but His Angels were Created as Servants with the sole purpose to unceasingly Praise and Worship Him and to Serve the Will of God; and Human Beings were Created in His Image, out of His Likeness to be His Heirs as the Children of God (Sons and Daughters of the Most High) and rulers of the earth.

Because we are created in the Highest Order, but for now a little bit lower than the Angels, God allows us (the Body of Yeshua-the Church) to judge the Angels on the Final Day of Judgement. We are Heirs to His Salvation and will take our place at that Final Day of Judgement, seated at the Right Hand of Yeshua ADONAI.

The Angels say, *"Holy, Holy, Holy is the Lord God Almighty!"*, while we (Humans) say *"Father you are Holy"*. A distinction between a Child of Inheritance and a Servant.

Angels are not to be worshiped nor honored in any way, they would be the first ones to tell you "Do not Worship me, Worship God".

There were some, a third of the Heavenly Host that rebelled and tried to overthrow the Throne of God. Everything that God Created has been given a free will so that they can express what is truly in their heart and by which God can Righteously pass Judgement on their actions. When Lucifer, one of the High Order Cherubim, who Covent the Throne of God, stirred the Rebellion to exceed beyond his bounds of authority, he became so impressed with his own beauty, intelligence, power and position that he began to desire for himself the honor and glory that belonged solely to God. So, God passed Judgement on him and the angels that join his rebellion and threw them out of the Heavenly Abode. He became known as Satan, the Destroyer and Father of all Lies, and God cast them all into the vast void of darkness that was to be later known as the physical universe. They were morphed into creatures of darkness (Demons) and could no longer share in the Presence of the Almighty and His Glory. And God created the Lake of Fire for them and their Eternal Torment, and this will be their final destination after the Final Judgement.

The Angels that were left in the Heavenly Abode that refused to rebel against God have been transformed into Holy Angels and pledge their Eternal Loyalty and Worship towards the One who Sits on the Throne in the Holy of Holies and is called the King of Kings and the Lord of Lords. God's Eternal Love is expressed through them as they revere His Honor and Holiness forever.

So, the distinction between God's Love for His Angelic Beings and us as His Children and Likeness of Himself, is summed up by what Jesus said in John 3:16, "*For God so loved the world, that He gave His only begotten Son, that whoever believes in Him should not perish, but have Eternal Life*". The meaning of this, which is so beautifully spoken by ADONAI is meant to reflect God's True Nature of Love which He has towards Himself and us as an extension of Himself. The angel's see us as a reflection of God's Image, but their dedication is only to

God in as much as their obedience is in fulfilling His Purpose. Therefore, God's love is fulfilled through us, and His Love is seen through the servitude of His Holy Servants, the Angelic Hosts.

22

God does not share in our Humanity
(Written in May 2018)

From Ken, who by the Grace of *Yeshua HaMashiach* and the Mercy He showed us all on the Cross, is giving testimony to what the Spirit of Truth is pronouncing to the world. As the Spirit reveals, it shall be given so that you may understand the Truth regarding El Shaddai and Savior *Yeshua HaMashiach*, who is the Mashiach of Israel and ADONAI Eloheinu, Amen!

YAHWEH does not share in our humanity, as if we are partners with Him in our human condition. Our humanity is sinful and keeps us at an impasse with His Holiness. From His perspective, you could say that we are Spirit Beings having a Human Experience and that experience is in a fallen state, which separates us from having direct interaction with Him in His Holy condition.

We share in His Righteousness through our faith in Yeshua ADONAI. The only way we can do this is through His Redemptive Power, which came about through the Eternal Sacrifice of Elohim as the Son of God (*Yeshua HaMashiach*), on the Cross at Calvary, on His Day of His Crucifixion and Death, as the Final Sacrifice to appease the Law of Atonement. This is where YAHWEH met man at an even plane. Where YAHWEH stood between Heaven, His Eternal Throne, and His Footstool (the Earth) where man resides.

He is not part of anything with us. If we share anything with Him, it is through His Grace and not because of what we do or have done for YAHWEH.

The fact that God became human was for our sake and it does not bind Him to us through our humanity; it binds us to Him through an Act of Faith. It was a Holy Act, not a humane occurrence.

He is the Creator, He is YAHWEH! The Father (ABBA) is YAHWEH; Yeshua ADONAI (the Son) is YAHWEH, the Holy Spirit (Ruach HaKodesh) is YAHWEH. He is One in the Same, Father, Son and Holy Spirit, One God (*ELOHIM*). He is Supreme Above All Things, everything is below Him, and nothing is above Him.

Sh'ma Yisra'eil ADONAI Eloheinu ADONAI echad
"Hear O'Israel, the Lord is our God, the Lord is <u>One</u>".

We are bound and connected to Him for everything through our faith and our confession of Faith in Yeshua HaMashiach.

He gives us through His Grace and Mercy, Ever Lasting Forgiveness and Propitiation of our sins, and the pathway to Eternal Life.

It is not because of our sacrifice that we receive anything from YAHWEH, it is by His Sacrifice that we receive All Things Eternal, and we come into the Presence of His Glory through our Faith. This faith is not ours to begin with, but His expression towards us of His Love. His Love is unconditional and sets no boundaries on how He can express it. The Essence of all life comes from Him.

The Testimony of Truth is that [1]"In the beginning, YAHWEH created the heavens and the earth" and that [2]"In the beginning was the **Word** (*Yeshua HaMashiach*), and the **Word** was with YAHWEH, and the **Word** was ELOHIM. He (*Yeshua HaMashiach*) was in the beginning with ELOHIM, and All Things were made through Him and without Him nothing was made that was made".

The Living Testimony is Him, *Yeshua HaMashiach,* Who Is, Who Was and Who Is to Come Again! The Alpha and the Omega, the Beginning and the End.

He is the King of Kings and the Lord of Lords. He is YAHWEH and shares all things with the Father (ABBA) as One in the Same. He is the Physical Evidence of the Unseen God.

It is impossible for us in our human condition to understand anything relative to what ELOHIM is, or to understand the purpose and manner in which YAHWEH moves through our humanity. Only Yeshua, who is our Advocate, can breech the void and chasm which separates us from YAHWEH, and it is the Ruach HaKodesh who gives us all understanding relative to what the Son (Yeshua ADONAI) wishes to reveal about El Shaddai and His Will to us.

Our Human Being is not just merely flawed, it is dead. Death engulfs us from our beginning of physical life (in the womb) to its end. It is the result of our sin nature and character to reject YAHWEH and absorb what surrounds us in this physical environment to which we were born into. Death is not a blessing, but a curse passed down by the judgement of El Shaddai due to the heart felt act of disobedience and blasphemy against the **Word** of YAHWEH (*Yeshua HaMashiach).*

From a God Virtue perspective, **Faith**, **Hope** and **Love** are what we consider to be acts of Godly Character when projected from our human venue. These are what have been given as the Three Great Virtues of ELOHIM; yet not one of them do we understand nor comprehend from YAHWEH's perspective. We attribute them only from our conception view and experience in a fallen state of being.

Faith is not just believing in something, but it is the Substance of YAHWEH and His Holiness. It is what YAHWEH projects throughout Eternity. It is the Virtue of Substance in which ELOHIM Created All Things in Heaven and the Physical Universe. It is the Power that YAHWEH projects to His Creation, in Heaven and on earth, and reacts to when the Creation requests action from Him. Faith is the kinetic energy which motivates ADONAI to take action on our behalf. From the human end, Faith is a Prayer (Request) that cries out to ADONAI, but from His end of receiving the Prayer in request, it is the Act of Grace which motivates El Shaddai to engage with a sinful Creation. In order for El Shaddai to interact with a sinful Creation, the Prayer of Faith must be received in a Holy manner. The entire point of sin in the Human Being is the result of Doubt. Doubt is the opposite of Faith. It is the motivator of Sin. Therefore, the Prayer (Request) must be made without any Doubt of conscience being (mind or manner) and projected to ADONAI in thanksgiving as if it has already been received. YAHWEH through His Grace, Honors Himself through responding to the Prayer of Faith. Grace is a Condition that shows Mercy, and Mercy is the result of showing Great and Unconditional Love.

Hope is not just waiting for YAHWEH to react and respond to our requests or believing that ADONAI will reveal Himself through an act of Grace which coincides with our Faith. Hope is the Virtue of Unconditional Love from YAHWEH and the belief that He keeps His Promises. It is knowing that ADONAI answers the Prayer of Faith, and His Justice will prevail even when we see no physical evidence of it happening. Hope believes that All Things are possible through the act of Faith and resides with the Faithful who are in *Yeshua HaMashiach*. Hope is what stands in knowing that a new day will dawn, and the darkness will pass away. Hope is the last Virtue standing on the battlefield of Faith and prevails against all doubt when overcoming the temptations from the enemy.

Love is not human by nature, nor is it substantiated through the Human Being. Love as a Virtue of YAHWEH is Unconditional and the substance of Holiness and Grace and the absolute condition of Forgiveness. Love is the Essence of YAHWEH in His Entirety. Love has no beginning and has no end; it is Eternal and holds no Doubt of Faith and no sin unaccountable. Love pronounces judgement on the unrighteous and shows Righteousness to the unjust. There is no situation where Love will not prevail and no means by which Love cannot be given. Love is the healer of sickness and the mender of the broken in
spirit and of heart. It ravages evil and decimates the enemies of Peace. It convicts the unbeliever and holds together the Faith of all who call upon ADONAI as their Redeemer. Love is the true Everlasting Force for YAHWEH is Love.

YAHWEH does not share in our humanity as if He is one of us, yet we are one with Him through the Acts of His Virtue and YAHWEH brings us into His Perfection when we acknowledge His Forgiveness of all our Sins and we receive His Free Gift of our Salvation through *Yeshua ADONAI*. At that moment we are truly one with ADONAI and share in His Kingdom and in His Presence Forever.

-23-
The Test from God
(Written in July 2013)

My Dearest Brethren, this message is not for the world, but for those who believe in the Way, the Truth and the Life. Receive this as a Blessing from God to further your understanding in Him.

In order for God to use us at His full intent, He must burn out the desire to rely on anyone else but Him. If fear is the way you react to this test, then God will bring fear to you, and this is what you will have to overcome in Faith in order to endure the test. If doubt is the way you react to this test, then God will bring doubt to you, and this is what you will have to overcome in Faith in order to endure the test. If rage is the way you react to this test, then God will bring rage to you, and this is what you will have to overcome in Faith in order to overcome the test. On the other hand, if questions are what you put before the Lord in this test, then God shall sustain the length of the test in order to bring out the answers according to the amount of Faith you impose. Be very careful in questioning ANY test that the Lord your God puts before you! Endure it and be silent after you have received your answer. Let the Lord burn out the temptation which is causing the test to be imposed. Remember, we are flesh and sin is part of the character of that flesh. Even though you have self-control, and the Will of the Spirit is in charge of your life, the flesh is part of your human nature. God is continuously testing our Faith, and in His own time is bringing us through the test in order for us to build endurance against the very thing that He has overcome Himself. When the test is first imposed by God we react by asking God...why? This is the first step in which we reach out to the Lord for help. It is also the most critical step in determining how long the test will last. Because God has insight into your heart, He also has insight to your true nature of Faith and the true nature of your flesh. The true nature of Faith is His Will, and the true nature of your flesh is your will (Human Nature). The test is to tear down your will and impose God's Will in your very nature so that you react to ALL things according to His Will. (By the way, this has no age limit or time duration associated with it).

This is why the flesh is being attacked? It is to bring us down, so that our will is under check, and to raise up Faith unto the Lord so that His Will shall be imposed and thus bring Him Glory.

God the Father has imparted in us the Great and Mighty Holy Spirit, who is revealing ALL the secrets about the Godhead. He is revealing to us Everything about Jesus (Yeshua Adonai) who sits at the right hand of the Father, who is the witness of ALL that God has to reveal of Himself to us. It is not enough for us to think that we belong to God and He loves us so much that all we need do is believe. Faith IS NOT measured by what you merely believe, but by what you endure. Jesus endured His Faith before the Father and retracted the judgment which falls on us because of sin (which is the lack of faith). Faith does not merely say, "Look...here I am". Faith shows itself through endurance by standing the test and thus giving Glory to God in the Highest! It is not because merely we say "I believe in Jesus that we are saved...it is because we believe in our hearts that we need to be saved and then call out to God for our salvation.

Remember, it is the prayer of Faith that God hears, and it is the test of endurance that God receives.

We must be tested...we must be put through the fire...**We must endure the test to the end!**

24

The Law of Tithing
(Written in March 2015)

I wonder how many Christians really understand the Law of the Tithing.

What almost every Church going Christian is taught or instructed, first and foremost, upon entering a religious organization or "Assembly of the Faithful", is how to give your money "Offering" to that organization or Assembly, it's the "Threat of the Tithe". It supersedes the teaching about Stewardship or preparing individuals on how to be Disciples of Christ and learn how to preach the "Good News" of Salvation to the world at large. You are quickly taught that Tithing is a Law of God and that it is a demand which is not revocable in any way; and in their desperation and greed, some of these Church Leaders / Elders / Pastors / Evangelist even go so far as to say boldly, that you are cheating God out of what is His and He will come after you and bring you to financial ruin if you do not give at least a tenth of your gross income to the Church. Under any secular setting or circumstance this is called "Extortion". What was given in Holiness to the nation that God had established as His own, has been extorted into a business and financial corporation called "the Church". The "Church" that Yeshua (Jesus) said He was going to build, is based upon the forthcoming Faith that was proclaimed by Peter (*Matthew 15:16-19*), was not to be an Institution, but the collective body of individuals that would come into the Faith and Knowledge in Him as

Lord and God, through the testimony given by the Apostles, then transferred by the testimonies of every individual thereafter who would become Believers...this is the "Church", the Body of Yeshua.

What the Tithing is and was given through the Law of Moses, was to the Nation (Children of Israel) as a building foundation to bring them under submission. It was to take a Chosen People whom God would make into His Holy Nation and make them understand that to Love the Lord your God, meant to give 100% of everything from your Heart, Soul and Being to God; this meant to be totally submissive to the Will of God, which He was ordaining through the Law. There was reward and punishment under the Law and this they were subjected. What most Christian's also don't realize (*basically because it is not taught in their Assembly*), is that until the time that Adam (through his disobedience and blasphemy) brought God's Judgment upon mankind, which until the Resurrection of Yeshua from the grave, the Law was imposed and had to be fulfilled in its entirety. Once ADONAI ascended to the Father and the Holy Spirit was sent to live with mankind (at Pentecost) and in every Believer of Yeshua, the Law was no longer imposed and the Church was to spread the Gospel of the Good News about Salvation through Faith in Yeshua ADONAI without bondage to the Law, and that Faith was the highest order and subsequent action to sustain our Salvation and that Propitiation of Sin was given under the same Faith that brought about our Salvation through Yeshua ADONAI.

There is no Law given to the Church about Tithing, nor

is there a requirement about bondage to the Law

required to Tithing. "Giving" is the Nature of God and should be reflective as the nature of every Believer in Yeshua. The essence of Love through God is in giving (John 3:16) but not bound through extortionists who hide under the shroud of godliness as Pastors, TV Evangelists, Healers, or Church Elders building Mega Churches at the expense of the Lord's Household (the Body of Yeshua).

One thing to remember, it cost NOTHING to receive the Forgiveness of our sins and our Eternal Salvation through Yeshua, it has already been paid for in Full by Yeshua! We owe God everything and we owe Him nothing in price for what He has done for us; the Law is not imposed on us! If we give, it must be given freely from our hearts, in Faith that has No Doubt, for Doubt is Sin.

Children of the Most High God, BEWARE of anyone who demands or extorts your money, your possessions or your Faith into guilt in giving to their Ministry or their Congregation for any reason whatsoever! YOU are not Bound to the LAW!!!

These are the Commandments which The LORD Commanded Moses for the children of Israel on Mount Sinai.

Deuteronomy 14:22-29

"Set aside a tithe—a tenth of all that your fields produce each year. Then go to the one place where the LORD your God has chosen to be worshiped; and there in <u>His Presence</u> eat the tithes of your grain, wine, and olive oil, and the first-born of your cattle and sheep. Do this so that you may learn to honor the LORD your God always. If the place of worship is too far from your home for you to carry there the tithe of the produce that the LORD has blessed you with, then do this: Sell your produce and take the money with you to the one place of worship. *Spend it on whatever you want*—beef, lamb, wine, beer—and there, in the presence of the LORD your God, *you and your families are to eat and enjoy yourselves.* Do not neglect the Levites who live in your towns; they have no property of their own. At the end of every third year bring the tithe of all your crops and store it in your towns. This food is for the Levites, since they own no property, and for the foreigners, orphans, and widows who live in your towns. They are to come and get all they need. Do this, and the LORD your God will bless you in everything you do."

Leviticus 27:30-

"And all the tithe of the land, *whether* of the seed of the land *or* of the fruit of the tree, *is* the LORD's. It *is* holy to the LORD. If a man wants at all to redeem *any* of his tithes, he shall add one-fifth to it. And concerning the tithe of the herd or the flock, of whatever passes under the rod, the tenth one shall be holy to the LORD. He shall not inquire whether it is good or bad, nor shall he exchange it; and if he exchanges it at all, then both it and the one exchanged for it shall be holy; it shall not be redeemed.'"

Numbers 18:21-

"Behold, I have given the children of Levi all the tithes in Israel as an inheritance in return for the work which they perform, the work of the Tabernacle of Meeting."

*   *   *   *   *

These excerpts from the Law of Tithing are not meant for the Church Age (the Time of the Gentiles), the time in which Salvation has been given to mankind, after the Day of Pentecost when the Holy Spirit (*Ruach HaKodesh*) was given to us. The Law is not given in this manner to the Church as it was to the Children of Israel and that Nation. The Church is not under that Law, but falls under God's Gracefulness, Redemption and Salvation.

Many false teachers will promote and extort the Law as being fully imposed on the Church and to the extent of capitalizing on all of the restrictive measures necessary to keep people bound to their will by guilt and doubt.

To the man, who has in faith, devoted his life to the preaching of the Gospel of Christ, there should be more giving of that individual than receiving! To those who are devoted to spreading of the Good News and message of the Redemption and Salvation of Yeshua ADONAI, let them sustain individual means of employment and give without receiving anything in return (Titus 1:7); but to the man who devotes his entire time to the teaching and ministry of Christ, the Church should sustain that individual with a fare wage for his work in the Ministry of preaching the Gospel of Yeshua (1Timothy 5:17-18).

This by no means should be under the Law of Tithing and should not be anything other than the loving donation of the Church (Body of Yeshua) wealth, given out of Faith and Devotion to the Ministry of Spreading the Good News of Yeshua ADONAI for the Salvation of the World.

We should not be giving out of the wealth of the Church to sustain individual congregations or pastoralists who do not intent to promote the evangelizing of every person into the public ministry of promoting and preaching the Gospel of ADONAI to the world, but rather keeps those persons bound to the comfort of a Home Church religious social event every Sunday and worthless meeting of a Pastors sermon and career-path ministry.

25

What is the Language of Heaven?
(Written in August 2012)

My Dearest Brethren, as I was at the Altar of my home this morning worshiping God and calling upon His Wisdom, the Spirit gave me a vision and a reminder of past encounters in which the Lord had given me specific answers to the questions I've had regarding the Things of Heaven. In this vision, the Lord gave me insight into the Language of Heaven and how God communicates All Things to us.

There is only One Method in which God communicates to us from His Abode, and that is through Faith.

This is not the kind of Faith in which we as human beings exercise, the kind we were taught or understand as we exist on the earth through what the Bible tells us; or by what the Church Leaders tells us, or by what we ourselves interpret the written word to mean. It is not a curriculum or agenda which has religious or theological meanings and interpretation. It is not at all seminary institutionalized dogma.

Faith is an Action!

Faith in Heaven is coming straight from the Throne of God, unabridged and full strength from The Holy and Righteous Source, which is The Word of God Himself. It is something that no man has ever experienced, since Adam fell from Grace, within himself. We, in human form, talk about faith as an escape from our sinful nature, which is caught up in doubt due to the sin that

190

resides in each and every one of us. For us, faith is a departure from sin and makes us one with God in acquiring His Favour, His Mercy, His Righteous and Graceful Nature.

Our act of Faith in calling upon the Word of God to Save us allows God to Save us from eternal death and ushers in Eternal Life to remove and replace what death was inside of us. Our dead human spirit is then transformed into a renewed Living Spirit from God Himself (The Holy Spirit) and we receive a New Name which is written in the Lamb's Book of the Living and the judgement of sin, and the outcome of its death is no longer against us. So, faith on earth is not the same Faith that resides and is existing in Heaven; it is but a small Image of what God uses to motivate His Power and Attributes to us.

Faith must be a heartfelt desire in order to motivate God's action; it cannot be a demand or calling upon for God to take action for us and give us what we want. This kind of motivation perpetrates doubt, which in turn promotes sin and disengages God from any motivation and may even bring God's judgement upon the request. As it is in Heaven, Faith is the language that speaks to His Heart and Motivates Him to act in our behalf under Righteousness through His Holiness.

So, language as it exists between humans on earth, is not the same language that exists in Heaven between God and His Created Beings. Language (the method of communication between man and man) is the form that was devised after man had fallen from God's Grace and was removed from His Abode on earth in Eden. In fact, man's language became so corrupt and divisive against God, that God had to separate man's method of communication between themselves by babbling it into many different tongues and human methods of language in order to keep man for being totally destroyed by God.

So, all the languages in this world are not so great because they are so unique and different, which gives men an opportunity to boast about their individual uniqueness and "Culture", but is in fact the result of man being so bad and sinful against the Holy God. There is nothing good about our diversity or the differences between our human languages as a Human Race in the Eyes of God. In the Abode of God in Heaven, there is No Diversity, there are No Cultures, there is No Race or Colour uniqueness, because there is <u>No Sin</u>!

What we hear through our ears and react to now is not the same things we will hear with our ears and react to once we are in the Abode of Heaven. Right now, Faith is the highest act that anyone can perform in worship towards God, Faith without doubt, Faith in Yeshua ADONAI (Jesus the Christ). It is the language between God and His Creation. In the same manner, Faith in the Abode of God, which will have no doubt inherently, is the only source of language by which God speaks to all of His Creation and they to Him.

There is no verbal communication as we know of it in our human existence on earth in Heaven. God speaks through His Method as Spirit and not flesh. There is no communication as we know it through verbal means, it is a One-on-One communication through Faith that relays all things to us as we stand in His Presence in His Abode of Eternity. We will be of one mind and one essence, Eternal in all things.

26

On the Edge of Eternity
(Written in October 2017)

The Human Race (Homo-Sapiens)-Mankind, created in the Image of God (Genesis 1:26-27), was made out of Spirit (Eternity) to be joined with Flesh, for a temporal moment of physical existence. All of us, from Adam forward, are Spirit Beings having a Human Experience. Although Sin has brought the Judgment of God upon us, that we all must suffer the Curse of Death, and our Flesh Body dies and returns to the earth it was originally formed from; the Spirit (Life Giving Force) inside of us returns to the Original Source in which it came from (Spirit-Eternity). As God's Will commanded a physical universe through His Word to appear out of Nothing; that which is unseen created all that can be seen; and All things (Past, Present and Future) came from One Source through Spirit, for God is Spirit (John 4:24), and All Things created in Heaven and in this physical universe, including us (mankind), already existed in the presence of God. The Will of God is that all these Things be manifested for His Glory and for His Purpose they exist. This makes Him the Sovereign Lord over ALL Things.

In the scheme of God's Purpose being executed and fulfilling His Sovereign Will, He had decided to create Man as the Highest Order of Creation and through His Own Image, He has placed Man above all things in the physical creation in order to Purpose His Will towards His Final Glorification and Worship. The Purpose of man's sin and the separation of man from a Holy God, was to edify the Sanctification and Mercy of the True Nature of God's Glory, to expressly show His Divine Nature of Love and Grace. In the Divine Presence of God's Holiness, the free-willed expression that He had given to Man, could not show His true expression of Mercy and Grace without the Highest Order of Creation having to submit themselves to God in obedience and supplication. Unless sin had abided in Man, mankind would not be able to understand the True and Divine Nature of God's Love and Mercy; and God would not be able to express His Sovereign Power over the Creation and demonstrate His True Nature of Everlasting Forgiveness and Clemency. God's sole Purpose of Creating Creatures out of His Purpose was for His Own Glorification and Worship and to demonstrate His Great Love towards that which is from Himself.

As each of us moves through God's Purpose in our Creation, we stand at a moment's notice of passing through the portal of this physical Human Experience into that State of Eternity. As the Highest Order of Creation, we will take our place either in the Presence of His Glory or in the Presence of His Eternal Judgment. This once again is under the Free Willed Expression of each person to decide the Eternal Path they will take; it is not a decision that God makes for us, nor is it one that He will take the Blame for if that individual finds themselves under the Judgment of His Wrath and the Path of Eternal Damnation. No one will be able to accuse Him or make an accusation that He did not give them the wherewithal to be redeemed, "*For God so Love the world that He gave His only Begotten*

195

Son (Jesus the Christ) so that everyone who believes in Him shall not die but receive Everlasting Life."

God has given Propitiation of ALL our Sins to Every Human Being through the Blood Sacrifice of the Lamb of God (Jesus the Christ). Now that God has prepared the way for us all by Forgiving and Forgetting our Sins, it is through Faith in Jesus the Christ, that everyone has the ability to receive Salvation and step into Eternity through the Portal of His Grace and Mercy.

Without this you will pass through the Portal of Eternal Judgment. The Lord Jesus says, "*Behold, I come Quickly!*" No one knows the day or the hour in which the Lord shall return or the time of your passing.

We are all constantly on the **Edge of Eternity**.

27

God Suffers our Faith
(Written in July 2017)

The Lord gave me a dream last night and in the dream a vision, as if He were talking to a great multitude of people. He stretched out His arms, and I could feel Power coming from Him like a great warmth and a feeling of Caressing Love all around me. "*In the Morrow*", said the Lord, "*In the Morrow, you will find Peace*"

Then the Lord disappeared from the vision and a bluish light appeared which gave me a feeling of wholeness and peace. The Holy Spirit began speaking to me; and it came to me that God watches, He witnesses our struggle through this life.
He watches us fall and get up, fall and get up, fall and stay laying.

He pleads with our weak faith, "*Be Strong!*"

He suffers our doubt, "*Have Faith!*"

He continues to call out to all the world, "*Believe in Me!*"

His message has not changed, "*IAM the Way, the Truth and the Life*"

His Spirit still has Command over our souls, "*Be Still and know that I AM GOD*"

His Everlasting Love shall forever be extended to everyone, "*Father Forgive them, for they know not what they do*"

His Mercy rescues us, "*Come to me, all you who are weary and burdened, and I will give you rest*"

He is the Word of God, "*Heaven and earth shall pass away; but My Words shall not pass away*"

He is the Lord God, "*Believe in God, also believe in Me*"...*for I and My Father are One in the Same!*"

For about 20 minutes the Lord was showing me one vision after another, these are too hard to describe; but another message from the Spirit was revealed to me; "*Take this down*", God has appointed a time when He will no longer Suffer our Faith and the Spirit shall no longer moan over the iniquity of mankind. We can safely say that we have an advocate (Yeshua ADONAI) who is constantly pleading in our behalf to God the Father (ABBA YAHWEH).

The only thing God sees through all of our human history (Past, Present and Future) is one event; and that event is himself on the Cross of Forgiveness and Mercy, pouring out His Love. That became the Propitiation of all our Sins. The Old Covenant where God covered the Sins through the Law of Atonement year after year after year; now God has finally and forever propitiated and eradicated sin through a New Covenant of Blood and Spirit, where Salvation may be obtained for all who proclaim in Faith the Son of God as that final and everlasting Lamb of God, through which Salvation may be obtained for all who believe and confess from their hearts with their mouths, that Yeshua ADONAI (Jesus the Christ) is Lord and God, to the Glory of God the Father!

There is but one transgression remaining which shall be the judge over all mankind on that Day when God shall resurrect all of the Living and the Dead and each person will stand before God and be Judged for what they have done. Anyone who did not receive the free and everlasting gift of Salvation through the Act of Propitiation by the Son of God, shall be condemned.

As I laid there contemplating what God was revealing, my spirit called out, "Oh Merciful God, how much longer will You Suffer our Faith?""

"*Not Much Longer!*", said the Spirit.

Someone reading this needs to make a decision, and now!

28

What is the Love of God?
(Written in January 2020)

From Ken, who is an Elder in the Church and by Faith proclaims this message to be one of truth and acknowledgement from the Spirit of ADONAI and is revealed as such for His Purpose.

It must be recognized that only through a spirit of humility and heartfelt worship and servitude does God honour our request to serve Him. ADONAI has again given to His imperfect servant insight regarding the mystery of God. As it is being given, may it be received.

To all who will read this: those who are in the Light and called to follow the Way, the Truth and the Life, sanctified by the Truth and redeemed by the Sacrifice of His Forgiveness; or to those that follow another path which leads them down dark corridors stumbling away from the Light and It's Truth, guided by the Ways of Deception and the Mouths of Liars, living in darkness and heading towards Desolation.

The Path of Righteousness is guided by the One who sits on the Eternal Throne of Glory and His Unconditional Love which is the Source of His Power and Emanates throughout all of His Creation in Heaven (His Abode) and on Earth (His Footstool). No conditions of our human sin nature or fallen state can alter how God Expresses His Love (Goodness) and Essence towards us. He is unwavering in Righteousness and Purity of Faith; His Power is Everlasting and Eternal.

The Essence of God is Spirit, for God is Spirit. Because He is Spirit, He is Eternal, with no beginning and no end. He does not have a physical body and by virtue of this, He is able to be Omnipresent and not limited by physical location. Because He is Spirit, He is also Omnipotent, having unlimited Power, able to do anything; He is not restricted by Himself, there is nothing above or beside Him in Majesty, Glory or Power. As well, because He is Spirit, He is also Omniscient, having unlimited knowledge, having no limits to His ability to know everything in His Creation (Past, Present and Future). Because of this, all Knowledge and Wisdom comes directly from Him to His Creation through His Spirit (Ruach HaKodesh) and He chooses what is revealed for the Purpose of His Glory and Honour. He is the Most High.

There is only One God (Elohim - ADONAI) and He is within Himself ALL THINGS, and All Things in existence, either in the Physical or Spirit Realm, came out of Him, Everlasting to Everlasting; and All Things continue to exist because of a Command that He has given, and which continues to go forth through Eternity according to His Will and for His Purpose which Glorifies Him alone.

The Love of God is not part of His Creation, it is not Human nor Angelic, it is not cosmic or metaphysical, and it is most definitely not a feeling or an emotional expression. The Love of God is Spirit and His Eternal Glory and Essence. All Things came about because of the Love of God and through The Word of God.

Unlike God, we (humans) have been created in the likeness of Him, through His Spirit. We are spirit beings having a Physical Human Experience. This is how we share in His likeness. It is the spirit which is inside of each and every one of us (the Life Force) that reflects the likeness of God, who is Spirit. This is why God said, "You are gods" (Ref: Psalm 82:5-7, John 10:34), which in the Written Testimony (The Bible) refers back to the beginning of what God intended when he created Humankind, "Let Us make man in Our Image, after Our Likeness." (Genesis 1:26) God is Three-Fold (Elohim) yet one God (ABBA-Father, Yeshua ADONAI-Son, Ruach HaKodesh-Holy Spirit). We as well are three-fold (Human) yet one person (Body-physical, Soul-mind, Spirit-Life Force-*which comes from God*). This is what ties us to Him in our order of Creation and our standing with His Eternal Purpose to exist as the Highest Order of His physical Creation. This was God's Will, that in His physical creation He Himself would have a physical representation of His Essence as a Physical Being and that Physical Being would be the highest order of His physical creation (Human-Man).

This also is how God would right the wrong that man did when he broke ties with his covenant through disobedience and blasphemy against His Spirit. God (Elohim) would depart from Spirit in order to join once again to man (through flesh) in order to bring restitution under the sanctification of the Law of Atonement and bring about the Propitiation of Sin, in order that all mankind could call upon God with a Heart Felt repentance and receive the Salvation of God and the Gift of Eternal Life in His Presence. This was accomplished through Elohim as the Word of God being manifested as flesh within the human creation in order to represent God as Man and thus bridge man to Him through the Love of God, by way of an Eternal Sacrifice appeasing the debt of man's sin owed to God and Final Atonement made through the Word of God (Yeshua ADONAI).

The misnomer and deception is that, we as humans think we understand what God is and what His Love embraces us with. The best we as humans can conjure up is what our human psyche is capable of in some form of metaphysical philosophy, religion, or occult mysticism, which totally relates to God in a mental or spiritual state of mind. There is no "Being" to God under that essence, God must become part of us in a humanistic manner in order for us to grasp what we think we are experiencing from either a supernatural or spiritual norm. It is a delusional state and even gives way to humans believing that they are somehow God, a deity in and of themselves. In order to fulfill this fantasy, they even try to project a deity-like appearance, dressed in holy robes or mystical attire, giving themselves titles of holiness and eminence, with actions of love and patience in how they conduct themselves with others, it's all "a show".

Unlike how God actually projects His Holy Eminence, they project their frailty of love in manners of goodness that somehow, they believe God reflects Himself to us through a show of Love. Outward and overt friendship and caring, emotional touching and hugging, happiness and uplifting speech and talk, physical attractions which eventually become obsession. All of this is of course temporal, because of the sin nature in all humans, we cannot continue this kind of charade for long sustaining periods of time. Our true nature of sin and corruption eventually comes out in front of the imaginary love of God we are trying to project. No matter how much you try to love, something in your sin nature will circumvent it and you will find yourself within an internal turmoil. A good natured and understanding personality is not necessarily a loving one. We always have conditions associated with our love and it is self-serving, self-gratifying, and selfish.

Because we are in a state of separation from God due to our physical sin and the nature of it (our Human Nature), God reveals Himself to us through sustaining Virtues. These have been expressed through three distinct Anthropomorphisms (Faith, Hope and Love) and the greatest of these is Love, because God is Love. But, because we cannot identify or relate to the specifics of what God's Love is or the conditions associated with the Unconditional Love of God, we have to try and associate them with what our sinful character and mind can understand and that is attributing them to human characteristics or behavior through what is called an Anthropomorphism. These characteristics are human and found throughout the Bible which frequently utilizes this approach, ascribing human-like physical qualities to God in order to give us a better understanding of what may be His Character and Actions by viewing them through a venue that makes sense to us in our physical and limited environment. In other words, we must bring God down to our level and in the process of doing that we limit ourselves to ever being able to express a true form of Worship towards Him. Nevertheless, if we did not approach our ability to understand God in this manner, then we would have no recourse towards any form of acquiring Faith or manifest Worship of any kind. In the sense that we express what God is in His Love, the Anthropomorphism for His Love is actually what we would see as the expression of His Goodness.

The one true overt statement that comes out of the mouths of the self-righteous or the misguided is for anyone of human origin to say, "let the Love of God come out of you" or "be one with God by allowing His Love to emanate from you to others", or the most self-servicing and ideological iconic statement which most Christian religious say, "be Christ-Like". It borders on blasphemy and the servitude of total self-righteousness. The Love of God is not passed to His human creation as if there is some kind of physical manifestation or gift which is poured out on the Body Faithful. If there is a goodness that is passed on from human to human through the act of "Love" which seemingly comes from God, then it is only due to the mercy and prominence of what Elohim has shown through the witness of the Godhead to the human creation by means of His Visitation to earth by the promise of Mashiach (Anointed One) who is Yeshua ADONAI (Jesus the Lord God).

It is by no means enough to just believe in Yeshua ADONAI (Jesus) without understanding that He is God manifested in mankind form and brings with Him the

Father's Spirit so that Salvation could be expressed through "The Love of God" and all creation once again be brought under His Sanctification. To believe in the sacrifice of Yeshua ADONAI and be redeemed by Him through the forgiveness of all sin and by the subsequent act of clemency and propitiation to allow by an act of faith (which has no doubt) on our part in receiving for the asking, both Eternal and Everlasting Life in His Presence through the Unconditional Love which He has Purposed in and of Himself according to His Will and for His Eternal Glory, which is that of ABBA YAHWEH (The Father God).

Elohim has given the expression of The Son (Yeshua ADONAI) to all of mankind as their Saviour and Advocate Representative and receive all things in the Purpose of what God the Father has freely given through the Essence of His Eternal and Unconditional Love. This stands apart from anything in all of His Creation. It is the Power and Prominence of His Spirit and Holiness.

It is an insurrection and utter blasphemy to compare anything in the Creation (in Heaven or on Earth) to be what God is or was or could be, except the manifestation of God the Son through Yeshua ADONAI (Jesus the Lord God). This is the only part of the Godhead that we can identify with and could ever imagine having a relationship with what is considered The Love of God.

The Love of God is Holy! The Love of God is His Spirit! The Love of God is Eternal!

To all who have given their life and worship to Yeshua ADONAI, be assured that He has written a New Name for you in His Book of the Living, and you shall have a place with Him in His Kingdom forever; for He has cast your sins from His memory (Presence) as far as the east is from the west and is your Advocate to the Father God (ABBA YAHWEH).

To all who have blasphemed and rejected the Word of God and His call for repentance and His Free Gift of Salvation, you shall not be found written in His Book of the Living, and on that Day when He shall Judge all of the Living and the Dead, you will not receive a place with Him in His Kingdom, but rather, on the Day that God shall Judge all things, anyone not found in the Book of the Living shall be thrown into the Lake of Fire where they are separated from God and in torment forever.

29

Being Christ-Like
(Written in June 2022)

From Ken, who by Faith has been called by the Great God and Saviour to be a teacher and is an Elder in the Church who declares the Truth regarding Yeshua ADONAI as being the Sovereign Lord and God. That His Name is above all other names, powers, and principalities in Heaven, on Earth and in the Underworld. That by His own Proclamation declares, "*IAM the Truth, the Way and the Life*"; and under no circumstance can any human declaration or decree be made that says He is not the One True God. For by proclamation from God the Father (YAHWEH), is that every knee shall bow, and every tongue shall confess that Yeshua is ADONAI to the Glory of God the Father, AMEN. May you open your eyes and your heart to the truth.

We cannot mimic God in any way, shape or form. To say so or even imagine it to be so is Blasphemy, and an overindulgence of our ego and is totally misguided. The measure by which God gives us to substantiate His Holiness is through Worshiping Him and the sharing of our Love for one another. It displays the Greatest Virtue of God as well as His Greatest Commandment to us, "*To Love the Lord God with all your heart and with all your soul and with all your mind. This is the greatest Commandment. And the second is like it: 'Love your neighbour as yourself'. (Matthew 22:37-39)*

And a new command He gave to all of us, *"Love one another; as I have Loved you, that you also Love one another". (John 13:34)*

There are many within the Church Communities (Religious Orders) who preach the false narrative of being "Christ-Like" or acting "Christ-Like", in the attempt for their members to pull back on their sin consciousness, and project something that they can never achieve. It demands that they conform to the Letter of the Law, and the examples of how Yeshua lived while He was conducting His Ministry on the earth. The narrative that reminds you of what actions to take in every decision-making process that you endeavour would be to ask yourself, "What Would Yeshua (Jesus) Do?" Now, that sounds like a good way to approach something that you may be in doubt with or always trying to be within the Will of God, but it does not reflect the Mind of Christ, nor how you would, could or should act like Yeshua.

What is "Christ-Like" is that you act like you act and with a consciousness that is guided by the Holy Spirit with all that you Think, Do or Say. Your actions are your own decision, but if you want to be in line with God's Will, then you should be driven by Faith (without any doubt), which is guided by the Holy Spirit. What does that mean, "to be guided by the Holy Spirit". It places the burden of Faith on YOU. That YOU as a Believer in Yeshua have made that decision to follow Him to the death of your sins and that you show Him Worship by way of your Faith. In order to do that successfully you must be under the guidance of the One Thing that projects the Mind of Christ, and that is the Holy Spirit. The Apostle John gave us direction with this by saying, *"But, the anointing which you have received from Him (Holy Spirit) abides in you, and you do not need anyone to teach you; but as the same anointing teaches you concerning all things, and is true, and is not a lie, and just as it has taught you, you will abide in Him."* (*1John 2:27*)

Man's attempt to project Holiness is to act a certain way, pray a certain way, say all the right words and phrases which are pleasing to the self-righteous and religious ear, and to adorn themselves in robes of honour which repel scandal away from their unholy deeds which are kept in secret.

Many believe their acts of holiness and Christian posturing make them "Christ-Like", above the fray of being cardinal and heathenistic. Being Christ-Like is not how you act, but how you believe, so that in return, how you believe projects your actions. If you wish to be in line with Yeshua, then consider engaging only with things that you can do in Faith (Without having any doubt). If you can't do something in Faith, then, Don't Do It!

It is through Faith that we pray for guidance and how to be a servant of Yeshua. We don't form an alliance or partnership with God by serving Him, but rather we worship Him through our servitude thus extending to Him our humility. God Loves a humble heart and a person of servitude and humility. This is the character that the Angels in the Abode of God have.

The mistake that people make with this kind of nature is to associate it with passivity and meekness. That Yeshua projected Himself as a Servant who was willing to die for all of us. That He always turned the other cheek and projected Love and Compassion towards everything and everyone. That this is the way in which we as His followers should also act and project ourselves in order to be "Christ-Like". Again, this narrative is a false one and gives the Believer no chance to Glorify God through our Faith. Yeshua wasn't just a Servant for us to receive our Salvation and Eternal Life through, but He was the fulfillment of all Righteousness and completion of the Law in order that Propitiation could be made for our sins and the debit of those sins be wiped clean in the Sight of God the Father. He fought a battle that was unthinkable while he was on the Cross being sacrificed for us. A battle was raging in both His flesh for all flesh, and in Spirit for all Spiritual domination. He was turning his cheek so that we would not have to. He was giving us
the Power to defeat Evil and the Powers of Darkness through His Servitude to God the Father.

There is an order by which things exist in this world, and that God has given it to us to overcome through His Righteousness and our faith. That there is Good and Evil, that there is Right and Wrong, that there is Lawfulness and Lawlessness, that there is Justice and Injustice, that there is Peace and Unrest, that there is Love and Hate, that there is God and an Adversary (Satan). Whatever God could project of His Nature to humankind, He did through His Son Yeshua, and now that He Sits at the Right Hand of The Father, He has all

Authority and Power given to Him, and we have the same Power and Authority through Him given to us through our Faith (which has no doubt). "*Most assuredly, I say to you, he who Believes in Me, the works that I do he will do also; and greater works than these he will do, because I go to My Father. And whatever you ask in My Name, that I will do, that the Father may be glorified in the Son. If you ask anything in My Name, I will do it*." (*John 14:12-14*)

So, there are no conditions in which God will not answer of prayer of Faith. We must realize that God works through our Faith, it is that kinetic energy that motivates Him to answer us, but it must be done with No Doubt in asking the request and it must be received as if He (Yeshua) has already given it. "*But let him ask in faith, with no doubting for he who doubts is like a wave of the sea driven and tossed by the wind. For let not that man suppose that he will receive anything from the Lord, he is a double-minded man, unstable in all his ways*." (*James 1:6-8*)

Therefore my brethren, be steadfast in your Faith, let nothing overcome or overtake you, let nothing do harm to you, (we are not to let someone beat us for the sake of a beating to withstand it), do not let evil win the battle, fight it with Faith that has no doubt, be humble in Faith but not in the manner you fight against evil, be steadfast and in all ways, be the same in manner as Yeshua was, that you may Glorify your Father who is in Heaven. AMEN!

30

What is the message in saying
"Jesus Loves You or God Loves You"
(Written in November 2022)

From Ken, who is an Elder in the Church and by Faith proclaims this message to be one of truth and acknowledgement from the Spirit of ADONAI and is revealed as such for His Purpose.

It must be recognized that only through a spirit of humility and heartfelt worship and servitude does God honour our request to serve Him. ADONAI has again given to His imperfect servant insight regarding the mystery of God. As it is being given, may it be received.

To all who will read this, the Path of Righteousness is guided by the One who sits on the Eternal Throne of Glory and His Unconditional Love which is the Source of His Power and Emanates throughout all of His Creation.

The Essence of God is Eternal, for God is Spirit (Everlasting to Everlasting); and His Greatest Attribute and Virtue that He extends to us is His Unconditional Love, which is sustaining us through our sinful human condition, by offering His Propitiation and Clemency of all our transgressions against Him, by sending the Messiah as the Lamb of God, Yeshua (Jesus) ADONAI (the Lord God), to give Final and Complete Atonement for all of the sins of mankind against Him (Past, Present and Future) in a way that would completely fulfil the Law of Moses and reconcile all humankind back unto His Presence. That Salvation and Everlasting Life is now afforded to all who would by Faith call out to and believe in His Namesake and acknowledge Him as Lord and God and would confess this openly from their hearts, shall be Saved. This Salvation brings great reward for all who would receive it, but it also brings great Judgement and Eternal Separation from God to all who reject it, for if you die in your sins and not found in the Lambs Book of the Living (Book of Life) when on that Final Day of Judgement, then you are cast into the Lake of Fire where all Sin abides for Eternity.

The format and protocols for converting Gentiles into Christians are not being taught necessarily to the proper context of the nature in which God is purposing His Creation and the interaction He is working through it. It is being taught from a Renewed Gentile perspective, as a Christian in the cultural setting of modern times and not from a Hebrew perspective, that the expressions of the phrasing of these words as transliterated or translated from Hebrew, Greek and Aramaic are interpreted properly in accordance with the way they were being used at the time and generation they were being spoken from. We must also be in-tune to the dialect and synonyms involved from the writer's language and cultural perspective, we cannot always interpret what the Gospels or any other referenced biblical writings have to say at face value to our current language and dialect, especially the English Language, and how the assembled Christian Bible was formatted into chapters and verses, which is not how the original text in Hebrew or Greek was formatted. Therefore, a lot of the formatted text, when read, overlooks the sustaining message from a previous verse or chapter and gives way to missing the complete message being given.

So, in the case of Atonement of Sins and transference into God's Propitiation and Everlasting Life through His Terms of Salvation, this is under the fulfillment of the Jewish Law of Atonement, known in modern times as Yom Kippur, where a sacrificial lamb would be the offering to fulfill another years' worth of God's Forgiveness and crediting the Debit to another time. Yeshua, 2000 years ago, became that Lamb of God for finally fulfilling the Law of Atonement, and it had to be in accordance to the Law of Moses, and paying all the accumulated debit into God's Propitiation (Clearing the Debt), which because of this, does not need to be replicated any longer for it is Everlasting in the sight of Father God (ABBA YAHWEH). Because Yeshua rose from the dead by the Power of God the Father as the Son of God (Resurrected) three (3) days later, thus conquering death and the curse that God imposed on Adam and all mankind, became the act that would give all of us who believe in Him as Lord and God, to acquire and sustain our Salvation and Eternal Life in His Presence forever.

The reality for everyone to understand is that God (Elohim) is Supernatural. Everything He does is beyond our understanding within and beyond this physical environment, and He has purposed that we can see into and commune with the Spiritual Environment as we live and function within this 3-dimensional physical state. He has complete control of all aspects of the Physical and Spiritual dimensions, and He does whatever He wants for His Purpose in those environments.

Originally, we were created beings, born of spirit (sinless) and made from the contents of the earth into flesh by the Creator God (YAHWEH) as the highest order of the Physical and Spiritual Creation (Created in His Image), to live in unity with Him as Holy Beings (Mankind) to be sons and daughters of the Most High. He wants us to Worship Him as such, and in return He would give us Life Abundantly and Eternity to stand in His Presence. But man chose freely to disobey and blaspheme a single Command of God to not partake in eating the fruit of the tree of the knowledge of Good and Evil. By being tempted and thus succumbing to the temptation and by doing this, it forced the Hand of God to pronounce Judgement upon mankind and all generations that would follow, by pronouncing death upon them and removing the Holy Spirit from the man and leaving him with a dead spirit (empty shell) inside that would eventually succumb to a physical death.

To say that "Jesus or God Loves You", is a Truth that is revealed by the Holy Spirit and should convict every Believer in saying "Amen". It has Eternal Power and Message in saying it; but in and of itself has no real impact if I don't know or understand WHY He loves us or why we should care in His message of Salvation or even care about the insult that I am perpetuating in a sinful nature toward God. How is it relevant to the non-believer at a personal level? This is where it is important to have a One-on-One personal Testimony regarding the Gospel (Good News), that the Name of

Yeshua (Jesus) is above all names and principalities in Spirit and in all of the Physical Creation. That all of mankind (Male and Female) are at a fallen state with the Holy God because of the transgressions of sin we have waged against Him, from the first man (Adam) passed down through every generation since then and that we need to be reconciled (Saved) to Him before death comes upon us, in order that we can stand before Him in Righteousness and all of Eternity. That the outcome of not receiving His Salvation means that we will be forever in His Judgement and cast away from his Righteousness and Presence forever, and this remains Notwithstanding.

Trying to stand as an individual witness by holding up a sign or telling someone that "Jesus Loves You", even that "Jesus Saves" isn't the Gospel (Good News). The statement is the absolute Truth, and the outcome of what was accomplished by Yeshua (Jesus), but it doesn't stand as a Testimony of the Good News because it doesn't explain why. As a Believer I can say "Amen" to that because my spirit bears witness to its Truth and my Faith stands in agreement with the Truth, but to a non-believer it is meaningless because they have no agreement in faith to what is being said or stated. Even adding a bible reference to the statement doesn't mean anything without the testimony of Faith to stand before it, they would not understand what it means because their spirit is still dead. Until they believe with their hearts and confess that Jesus is Lord, to the Glory of God the Father, they are not Born Again and have not received the Holy Spirit which reveals these Truths to them. It's because the Gospel is

217

not being preached in a way that reveals the whole Truth of why Yeshua (Jesus) Loves us. So, what is the "Good News"? **The "Good News" is that our Captivity to Sin is Over!** And why is that? It's because God Himself had to Save us, because nothing that we could do ourselves could meet the requirements demanded by God to do so.

It's through our testimony of Faith that we share the Good News, not the testimony of how we personally got saved or the story of our personal conversion or circumstances that brought us into Salvation through acceptance or coercion of our own doing, but by Faith through the Testimony which the Holy Spirit conveyed to us that brought about our conversion to the Truth that Yeshua (Jesus) is ADONAI (the Lord God). We then believe and confess this Truth as a Born-Again Believer through a Renewed Spirit to the whole world and our Testimony now stands before us.

That we are Spirit Beings having a Human Experience and it is temporal and are in need of reconciliation with God.

That we are all born into sin and death because of our inherited sin nature through our flesh which opposes the Holiness of God, and that God has afforded every human His forgiveness of all their sins as the atonement to our sin nature and has given propitiation through His Grace and Mercy. That we now have a way for every human to come into His Presence by calling out to Yeshua (Jesus) and opening the door to our heart and receiving Him as ADONAI (Lord and God), thus He affords them Everlasting Life and acknowledges them in the Lambs Book of the Living (Book of Life).

This is why we can say with a loud voice and assured testimony that "

Yeshua ADONAI Loves You!

31

The Glory of God and His Holiness
(Part I & II)
(Written in November 2018)

Part I
The Glory of God in the Highest

I wish to humbly begin by proclaiming, that by no means do I want to pretend that I have any exact knowledge or understanding to either the fullness of the Glory of God or His Holiness, nor should it be said that any man (excluding the Living Son of God-Jesus the Christ) ever created and born by natural means into the fallen state of this world has ever seen It either (Past, Present or Future). In many references throughout the Holy Bible, the translation of the phrases "His Glory" or "His Glory was revealed", is in reference to His Presence or manifestation of His Essence. The closest thing man has experienced is the Essence of God's Glory or Holiness which was revealed to only one man and that was Moses and not Face to Face, but from His Backside. Not even with Abraham, the Father of all Nations, did God reveal Himself in such fashion. Any documented references of manifestations or visitations by angels did not reflect the Glory of God, but only the Essence of Him; and any reference to what appeared to be the Son of Man or The Lord in human form, like with the visitation at Abraham's tent of the three angelic beings dealing with the sins of Sodom & Gomorrah, or with the Transfiguration of Jesus (*Matthew 17:1-2*), is in fact a suppression of God from His True Glory down to a lower level of earthly incarnation in order to meet us at our level. The human form of God does not reflect His *Shekinah*, but rather Glorification between the Father and the Son in Their relationship as the Godhead, by which the Son could then be seen as reflecting the Glory of God. In all instances, it is suppressed beyond our understanding in order that He may appear in the form of the highest order of creation (Human) and communicate to us. If He did not filter or suppress His Glory in His appearance to us, our flesh body, due to its inherent sin nature, would burn up at the very sight of Him. Thus, His sustaining Truth and Knowledge of His Glory is through the Holy Spirit and manifested through the Body of Christ (the Church).

God's Glory, whatever that is and whatever form it may be in Heaven, is something that no man has ever seem. It is something that exists and resides in the Abode of God; and by His Perfection, Purity and absolute Holiness, cannot be shared with any man or creature under the creation. This includes many of the Angelic Beings that reside in the Presence of God and worship Him relentlessly since the beginning of all creation in Heaven. The Seraphim (Seraph), who are the highest order of the hierarchy of angelic beings, are the closest to the Throne of God, in the direct Presence of God and they reflect the Essence and Power of God's Glory on them and even through them. They were created with six enormous wings, two that cover their legs, two that cover their face and two that they fly with (*Isaiah 6:2-3*). They are called the "Fiery Beings", because of their fiery appearance reflecting God's Eternal Glory. They fly around the Throne singing Praise to the Most High, "Holy, Holy, Holy is the Lord God of Hosts, the ruler of Heaven and Earth", "Holy, Holy, Holy, is the <u>Lord God</u> Almighty, who was and is and is to come!". They constantly sing Praises that reflect the continuing essence of what the Glory of God is expounding through His creation, both in Heaven and on Earth, the never-ending expanse of what God's Glorified Being is and the awesome and Eternal Power that emanates through Him.

Even Adam, in his created state of perfection, did not see the Glory of God in full measure. In the Book of Genesis, it reveals that God always called out to the man (Adam) and the man would reply. It mentions that God brought every living creature He had made to the man so he could name them. Adam walked with God, had communion with Him, but not a physical manifestation of being, rather though the Holy Spirit that God had breathed into Adam, where at the moment He gave Life to the Man, and he became a Living Being.

What we bring to Him through our Faith in Jesus the Christ is Glorification (Praise and Honour), reverence to His Holy Name. In our finite minds of only being able to consider understanding and discovery through the physical means afforded by God, in regard to His physical creation, we've lost what that first man had, the ability to interact with the Holy God without restraint from sin, the Holiness of thought and being (Spirit). Can you even imagine what it must have been like for Adam to be in a state of perfect being, filled with the Holy Spirit, not having the knowledge or understanding of "Good" verse "Evil", completely innocent and pure (naked) in thought and existence before God, to have been thrusted into such knowledge through the act of disobedience and in the Sight of God, blasphemy. To have to go from Communion with God, into the His Judgement. To pass from Life into Death, to have the Holy Spirit depart from him and be an incarnate of sin (separation from God in perfect standing and purpose). Instead of knowledge and understanding, he received confusion and doubt as to his purpose and being. The essence of God's Glory was in the background, and the knowledge of evil was now prominent, and death was pronounced and lurking in the future for him and all mankind.

Part II
What does it mean that God is Holy, Holy, Holy

The phrase "Holy, Holy, Holy" appears twice in the Bible, once in the Old Testament (Isaiah 6:3) and once in the New Testament (Revelation 4:8). Both times, the phrase is sung by heavenly creatures (Seraphim), and both times it occurs in the vision of a man who was transported to the Throne of God: first by the prophet Isaiah and then by the Apostle John. Before addressing the three-fold repetition of God's Holiness, it is important to understand what exactly is meant by God's Holiness, He is Holy (*Kadosh*).

The Holiness of God is the most difficult of all God's attributes to explain, partly because it is one of His essential attributes that is not shared inherently by man.

We are created in God's image, and we can share many of His attributes, to a much lesser extent of course—love, hope, faithfulness, mercy etc., but some of God's attributes, such as omnipresence, omniscience, and omnipotence, will never be shared by His created beings. Similarly, Holiness is not something that we will possess as an inherent part of our nature; we only share in Holiness with our relationship to Jesus the Christ. It is an *imputed* Holiness. Only in Christ do we "become the righteousness of God" (2 Corinthians 5:21). God's Holiness is what separates Him from all other beings, what makes Him separate and distinct from everything else. God's Holiness is more than just His perfection or sinless purity; it is the essence of His "Otherness," His Transcendence. God's Holiness embodies the mystery of His Awesomeness and causes us to gaze in wonder at Him as we begin to comprehend just a little of His Majesty.

Isaiah was a firsthand witness of God's Holiness in his vision described in Isaiah 6. Even though Isaiah was a prophet of God and a righteous man, his reaction to the vision of God's Holiness was to be aware of his own sinfulness and to despair for his life (Isaiah 6:5). Even the angels in God's presence, those who were crying, "Holy, Holy, Holy is the LORD Almighty," covered their faces and front covering with four of their six wings. Covering the face and front covering no doubt denotes the reverence and awe inspired by the immediate presence of God (Exodus 3:4-5). The Seraphim stood covered, as if concealing themselves in recognition of their inability to stand in the presence of the Holy One, but only reflect His Glory; and if the pure and Holy Seraphim exhibit such reverence in the presence of YAHWEH (**IAM**-*Ehyeh*), with what profound awe should we, polluted and sinful creatures, presume to draw near to Him! The reverence shown to God by the angels should remind us of our own presumption when we rush thoughtlessly and irreverently into His Presence, as we often do because we do not understand His Holiness.

John's vision of the Throne of God in Revelation chapter 4 was similar to that of Isaiah. Again, there were living creatures (Seraphim) around the throne loudly crying, "Holy, Holy, Holy is the Lord God Almighty" (Revelation 4:8) in reverence and awe of the Holy One. John goes on to describe these creatures giving Glory and Honor and Reverence to God continually around His throne. Interestingly, John's reaction to the vision of God on His Throne is different from Isaiah's. There is no record of John falling down in terror and awareness of his own sinful state, perhaps because John had already encountered the risen Yeshua (The Christ) at the beginning of his vision (Revelation 1:17). Yeshua had placed His hand upon John and told him not to be afraid. In the same way, we can approach the Throne of Grace if we have the hand of Christ upon us in the form of His Righteousness, exchanged for our sin at the cross (2Corinthians 5:21).

But why the three-fold repetition "Holy, Holy, Holy", (called the *Trihagion*)? The repetition of a name or an expression three times was quite common among the Jews. In Jeremiah 7:4, the Jews are represented by the prophet as saying, "The temple of the Lord" three times, expressing their intense confidence in their own worship, even though it was hypocritical and corrupt. Jeremiah 22:29,Ezekiel 21:27, and 2 Samuel 18:33 contain similar three-fold expressions of intensity. Therefore, when the angels around the throne sing or cry to one another, "Holy, Holy, Holy", they are expressing with force and passion the truth of the Supreme Holiness of God (El Shaddai), which expresses His Awesome and Majestic Nature.

In addition, the *Trihagion* expresses the Triune Nature of God, the three Personages of the Godhead, each equal in Holiness and Majesty. Yeshua ADONAI (Jesus the Christ) is the Holy One who would not "see decay" in the grave, but would be resurrected to be exalted at the right hand of God (Acts 2:26;13:33-35). Yeshua is the "Holy and Righteous One" (Acts 3:14) whose death on the cross allows us to stand before the throne of our Holy God unashamed. The third Personage of the Trinity—the Holy Spirit—by His very name denotes the importance of Holiness in the essence of the Godhead.

Finally, the two visions of the Seraphim around the throne crying, "Holy, Holy, Holy", clearly indicates that God is the same in both Testaments. Often, we think of the God of the Old Testament as a God of Wrath, and the God of the New Testament as a God of Love. But Isaiah and John present a unified picture of our Holy, Majestic, Awesome God who does not change (Malachi 3:6), who is the same yesterday, today and forever (Hebrews 13:8), and "with whom is no variableness nor shadow of turning" (James 1:17)

32

Punishment under the Law verses Forgiveness through Mercy
(Written in March 2013)

The Law was not given to bring about Forgiveness nor Salvation; it is a conviction of Rules and Regulations on how to live under the suppression of Sin. The Law shows us that we can Never do enough Good to please God, so the Law was a means by which God allowed His People (Israel) to keep on living by performing its edicts under obedience. If you did not obey, you were punished, even unto death, if you obeyed you would live long in the Land that God had provided. Even though the Law was prevalent at one time and would stand forever before God because He commanded its entirety, it would be superseded by the Heart of God's Love and Mercy through Forgiveness into Salvation.

This would be done as prophecy foretold through the Messiah, the Son of God, **Jesus the Christ**. When the appointed time finally came for His appearance, Messiah would redeem all of mankind (every nation and tribe) and forgive all sin for everyone forever (past, present and future). You could say that the people living under the Old Covenant, from Abraham to the moment of the Death of Jesus on the Cross, were living on Credit towards the Mercy and Forgiveness that The Messiah would fulfill by His Death on the Cross and take the Sins of the World unto Himself by becoming the Sacrificial Lamb of God. When Jesus said, "It is Finished! "or "It is Fulfilled!", He was referring to the satisfaction by God the Father to be completely and forever satisfied with the Blood Sacrifice of Atonement under the Old Covenant (The Law), to a New and Forever Lasting New Covenant sealed with the Blood Sacrifice of Propitiation.

The Old Covenant under the Law gave Atonement for Sin (Covering the Sins), but not the removal of Sin (Leviticus 23:27-28) (Leviticus 16:1-34). It was an act that had to be repeated every year after year, after year, under the Law. At the moment Jesus gave up His life on the Cross, ALL Sin was now Propitiated and the Judgement under the Law Removed. Mankind was now under the Grace of God and the Mercy of Forgiveness; with the Door of Salvation available to anyone who would receive it by way of Faith, through a Heartfelt Confession and Repentance of their Sins being taken away by the sacrifice of Jesus the Christ; and that by Faith they believe in Him as Lord and God will receive Salvation and Everlasting Life (1John 5:19-20) (Romans 10:9-10). Salvation and Everlasting Life was accomplished for us through the Death and then Resurrection of Jesus three days after His Crucifixion.

You must remember that we are not talking about just any man here, nor is this some kind of fictional story made up to be some kind of fulfillment of a fantasy or religious order. We are talking about the Almighty God, Creator of ALL Things in Heaven and this entire universe. We are talking about the real Supernatural Being. We are talking about the Most High God coming to Mankind in order to Save us and bring us out of the bondage of Sin (which isolated us from Him to begin with by the first man-Adam); and Judgement of the

Law, into the Highest Order of His Creation. It is so absolutely incredible, that God wants to commune with us so deeply and lovingly and eternally, that He would take it upon Himself to be our Sacrifice in order to put us right with Himself. It was not God's fault that man chose to sin against Him; He is Holy and beyond our conceptual understanding of what this is or entails in order to stand in His Presence. Since the moment that the first man sinned against the Lord God and forced the Holiness of God to pass Judgement on the man and all of his off-springs, God has been bringing mankind back unto Himself. His Purpose for Salvation was set in motion and fulfilled through Himself in the Second Person of the Godhead as the Son of God, **Yeshua ADONAI**.

It is evident that God's Ways are not our ways, and He is above our purpose or understanding. His Purpose to completion is not something that we can completely envision or understand; yet the Lord has always told us through His Spirit and Word that He is our Redeemer and our Salvation. The Law was just a pretense to the Action that God was taking to bring sin under control and to show how wonderful His Mercy is in comparison to Judgement; and how Great God is in His Everlasting Purpose and Love for mankind.

Faith shall ensure this; Faith shall sustain us, and Faith shall be the force which motivates God to hear us and take action to Glorify Himself and Bless us.

33

What is the Gospel?
(Written in November 2024)

My Dearest Brethren, so many of you are weak in the Faith and lack Knowledge and Wisdom in preaching what is the Truth in regard to the Good News, that through Yeshua of Nazareth, The Son of God, Who is, Who Was and Who is to Come Again, ALL of Mankind has been given Clemency of their Death Sentence and the Judgement of God, because He has redeemed us Forever, by being what God (ABBA YAHWEH-the Father) considers as "The Eternal Sacrifice" for all of our transgressions against Him. The Son of God Yeshua ADONAI (Jesus the Christ) stood in our place, between God and Man, and took unto Himself our Transgressions (Sins) against God and has completely Forgiven those transgressions by fulfilling what the Law of Moses decreed as the Atonement Sacrifice. He became that Eternal Sacrifice so that once and for all, the Law would be completely fulfilled and no longer would our Transgressions against God need Atonement (Covering Over), but He would give Propitiation (Payment in Full) and complete Forgiveness of all our Transgressions, Forever! This is the fulfillment of what King David said in Psalms 103:11-12 concerning the Messiah taking our Transgressions and casting them away from Him, as far as the East is from the West.

The Command of Yeshua, "to take this Gospel to the Ends of the Earth" by His Apostle's and then to all the Disciple's that would come afterwards through their testimony, would become the Foundation of the Church through the Ages. This is the reason He sent us the Ruach HaKodesh (Holy Spirit), who is the Teacher and Reveals the Truth about all that Yeshua is to humanity and to be The Witness of the Truth, which is that, Yeshua ADONAI!

Starting with those men who lived and witnessed first-hand, Yeshua ADONAI as He walked this earth as the Son of God (God in Flesh-Man God) and witnessed His Glory and Power as given by the Father to prove beyond any doubt, that He was God and Messiah, who was coming to finally bring mankind back into "Good Standing" with God, just as Adam was before His fall into sin. So, God was bringing in Full Circle what He had originally set forth for His Creation in the Garden of God to begin with.

The reason so many of you are weak in Faith is because it is dumbed up by religious dogma and false teaching; that the Church here on earth has become what Yeshua said it would be in this last generation, just before His return, the Church of Laodicea (Revelation 3:14-21). Leaders within the Church are like wolves in sheep's clothing, sinister and evil in leading the Fold of Yeshua in a misguided direction in order to control the Church in their fashion and profit, thus projecting a False Gospel and illegitimate doctrines, which the world can use as a contradiction to the real Gospel of Yeshua.

It is for each of us who are in Yeshua ADONAI, not just Church Leaders (Pastors, Evangelists, Missionaries and Teachers) to be a witness of the Truth; to be the physical extension of the Good News that He proclaimed and still does through the Ruach HaKodesh by means of the Church (the Body of Yeshua).

Many believe that the Gospel is about His death on the Cross and the Forgiveness of Sins, but that is just part of the Good News, the rest is that when YAHWEH God Raised the Son from the Grave (Death), He did so into Eternal Life. He had now and forever given to mankind the Greatest Gift and the Means to Eternal Life. That those who will put their heartfelt Faith in believing that Yeshua is The Resurrection and the Life and will call upon His Name and receive by Faith, not only the Forgiveness of their Sins (Transgressions), but their Salvation, that they will also be given Eternal Life through Faith in Yeshua ADONAI and a share in His Kingdom Forever.

Why is this such a pressing issue with Christianity? Why is there such a need to be Saved?

It is estimated that today, only 1% of the total Global Body of Yeshua is active in a Gospel Ministry, which is promoting the spreading of the Gospel of Yeshua. It is also estimated that 31% of the 7.4 billion people in the world consider themselves to be Christian through association to a religious order. In the 2020 USA Census, 45% of the Christian Church consider themselves to be within the Gospel definition of "Born Again", and the percentage is much less in the World-Wide Christian Community.

This means that the overwhelming majority of the "Body of Yeshua" are either not practicing their Faith or are complacent in showing up on Sunday and putting their Rear-Ends in pews watching the "Big Show" or just listening to a Pastors Sermon on a verse of Bible Scripture with no conviction of participating in the Command of Yeshua to Spread the Good News throughout the Ends of the Earth.

The Scriptures are not the "Good News"; The "LAW" is not the "Good News"; the Birth of Yeshua was not the "Good News" (although it was the event that led to it). **The "Good News" is that our Captivity is over, our Captivity to Sin!** We are no longer Enemies of God, but rather through Faith in Yeshua ADONAI, we are put Right with God and become His Children and are Saved from the Judgement of Eternal Damnation. This is something that is Life itself; for every person born (Past, Present & Future) will someday die and we all go to one of two places designated by the Creator. When this life ends...It ENDS! There is a follow-on Eternal transition that takes place afterwards.

The funny thing is that the vast majority of Pastors and Church Leadership don't want that kind of teaching or conviction to be promoted. What they have is a career path mentality and their congregation is the pathway to maintaining that job security. It's not to bring more people to ADONAI and His Salvation as it is to bring more people into the local Church Congregation and grow that venue. The Altar Call is not necessarily to benefit the sinner into Salvation as it is to get persons into the Congregation that have similar belief and loyalty thus sustaining the program agenda without opposition.

As the Children of the Most High God and Receivers of His Salvation to Eternal Life, our absolute conviction to our God should be beyond doubt, that we are Servants to Him more than we are Recipients. Our Love towards His Unconditional Love for us, should be one of utmost devotion, and that devotion should always be unwavering towards the testimony of His Sacrifice and Free Gift that He has secured for all mankind (every human being).

The pressing issue and need for preaching the Good News to all of humanity is that every one of us has a destiny towards an end, we are all going to die. That death has a sting to it in our existence, and no one knows the day or the hour or the circumstance in which this physical life will end. The impunity of this life force within each of us is Eternal, so when facing this destiny at its end, we are entering into an Eternal Cross-Roads of either the Grave (Darkness) or the Presence of God (Light). The decision of that destiny is not after you die, but before. It is by the Pleasure of God, that no one go into Darkness, but receive the Salvation afforded through Yeshua ADONAI, for there is only One God and One Intercessory between God and Man, and that is Yeshua ADONAI. This is the Complete "Good News" or Gospel. **There is No Other**.

34

What is the purpose of Water Baptism and is it necessary to receive Salvation in Yeshua
(Written in July 2019)

My Dearest Brethren and Children of the Most High God: From Ken, who is an Elder and Teacher in the Church of Yeshua Adonai. My ABBA YAHWEH give you understanding of this Letter to the Church (Body of Yeshua), so that you will be filled with the Truth and not let anyone deceive you in your Faith!

In the last 2000 years, throughout the history of the Church Age, there have been many false teachings based around misinterpretations and mis-transliteration to the written language of the New Testament.

The consensus of Pastors, Evangelists or Teachers who have been through the indoctrination and education of a Seminary and or Christian Institution; and especially those individuals who are Ultra-Religious and under restrictive doctrines and dogma, do not necessarily give them the wherewithal of being exposed to the Truth regarding the proper interpretation of the four (4) Gospels and associated Letters, which combined, make up what we use as the written New Testament and Testimony regarding Yeshua ADONAI (Jesus the Lord).

In every instance where misinterpretation abides, the main reasons are relevant for not including within the interpretation, the historical Jewish Traditions, Cultural

Lifestyles and Religious Implications of the times in which the Gospels and associated Letters were written.

Our Western Culture does not give allowance for understanding the Jewish Culture or Society associated to the written text at the time the four Gospels were written; and the Linguistics of the English Language which interpreted the Greek, Hebrew and Aramaic Transliterations was far from being accurate in so many instances in the Bible. Many scholars will say that the King James interpretation done in 1611AD is by far the most accurate account of what was transliterated from the original Hebrew, Greek and Aramaic Text, but it is not exact, which leaves many of the phrases and words open to misinterpretations. This has led to the development of a Concordance, which is a cross-reference of words and phrases used in the Bible that associate the true meaning of the English translated word to the original Greek, Hebrew or Aramaic word as transliterated. The Concordance does not intend to relate any of the original words or phrases to a cultural basis, so that the use of the words in the phrases apply to the understanding of the true meaning as related to the time in which the culture and social traditions would apply them. The Concordance gives what the word could or would mean under standard English interpretation in a linguistical context, which may not be the true meaning or intent being conveyed.

In many regards, theological intercession and tradition takes place over cultural and historical fact, as well as the Bible being regarded and reverenced as the "Infallible Word of God" in order to make up for these inconsistencies: instead of it being actually what it is, the written testimony of these facts, which would render it under interpretation as well as factual evidence to what the Word of God, Yeshua ADONAI (Jesus the Lord) intended and the Holy Spirit reveals to us in Truth and Testimony.

One such example of this is on the teaching of Baptism and three basic questions which have been argued regarding this:

1) Is it necessary to be Baptized in Water in order to receive Salvation through Yeshua?
2) Does an individual need to be Baptized in Water before they can be considered Saved?
3) Is Baptism in Water the same as being Baptized in the Name of the Father and of the Son and of the Great and Mighty Holy Spirit?

The answer to all three of these questions and any others similar to this, is Absolutely Not... NO!

First, a little History Lesson on the Jewish Traditions and Obedience to the Law:

It is by deliberate tradition that the Church rendered itself under the Law of Moses and Water Baptism in accordance with the Jewish Traditions and Religious Order during the First Century when the Apostles in Jerusalem started the Church there, under the leadership of James, the half-brother of Yeshua. Because they were under great persecution, fear and condemnation, they sought after those who wanted to be part of their group, who were all Jews. They had been given no guidance on how to begin building what

Yeshua called His Church.

Their fellowship was built around the only Standard they knew and was promoted by ADONAI (the Lord) during His Ministry while on earth, which was to the Law of Moses and the traditions of their Jewish upbringing. One of these Traditions was Water Baptism.

After the Maccabean Wars (~167BC - 160BC) led by Mattathias the Hasmonean (One Hundred and Sixty years before Yeshua of Nazareth and Yohanan (John the Baptist) came into the world, there started a tradition whereby all Jews would show their allegiance to the Law of Moses and be reinstated to it through the act of being Baptized in Water; it was a Cleansing Ceremony. As well, this was also the way in which Non-Jews (Gentiles), would be allowed to convert into the Jewish Faith (Judaism) as a show of their conversion and ritual cleansing; this became part of the Pharisaic Law and as such, made part of the Common Law of Cleansing and prescribed Ritual therein. In this same time period, the Jewish festival of Hanukkah came about which celebrates the re-dedication of the Temple following Judah Maccabee's victory over the Seleucids and became a Rabbinical tradition, as did Water Baptism which was adopted as a mandatory part of this Tradition and indoctrinated as part of the Law. When Yohanan (John the Baptist) began his ministry, he did so under the Jewish Tradition which followed the Law of Moses and the Rabbinical Tradition of Water Baptism Cleansing in order to prepare the way for the Messiah, who would follow after him. Before Yeshua began His Earthly Ministry, He went before Yohanan so that He fulfill the Order of Water Baptism according to the Rabbinical Tradition. Even though John claimed that he needed Baptism by Yeshua, ADONAI said, "We must fulfill all Righteousness", and so John Baptized Him in Water proclaiming His Righteous standing and dedication under the Law of Moses and Rabbinical Tradition.

According to the Purpose that the Messiah was to fulfill under Jewish interpretation of the Scriptures; Yeshua, at His Appointed Time and Visitation, was not going to fulfill. His Purpose according to what God the Father had appointed, was for the Son of God to prepare "The Truth, The Way and the Life" for all mankind to be forgiven their sins (now and forever) and to fulfill all Righteousness under the Law of Moses, thus allowing Yeshua to Propitiate the Law under Grace and then order "Faith" to be the Standard in replacement of the Law.

Yeshua, being Elohim (2nd Proponent of the Godhead - God in the Flesh), was coming as both Prophet and Messiah of Israel in order to fulfill all righteousness under the Law of Moses according to the Holy Scriptures. This would allow Him to stand between God and Man as their Saviour (The Son of God) as well as Advocate and fulfill the Prophecies, thus become the Sacrificial Lamb of God in accordance with the Law of Atonement; and give Propitiation of Sin for all Mankind Forever. This replaced the Law of Moses with the Law of Faith through Grace. God once and for all gave Clemency to the Atonement of Sins and Paid in Full the

Credit which had been accumulating through the Law of Atonement.

Meanwhile, the Church in Jerusalem was becoming more and more embedded into the Law of Moses and making any new members coming to Yeshua ADONAI conform to the Strictness of the Law including Circumcision and Water Baptism. Unless the members acknowledged their allegiance to the full Law and Traditions, they were not allowed to become part of the Body of Yeshua (the Church) and considered unsaved.

The breakaway of this is when Saul of Tarsus (later known as Paul) was commissioned by Yeshua Himself to become the Apostle of the Gentiles and begin forming the World-Wide Church that we are today. The message was that "Faith" supersedes all acts and works under the Law, and that we are no longer bound by the Law. That any new converts being brought into the Church should not be bound by the Law of Moses or the Jewish Rabbinical Traditions.

One of the most used verses within the New Testament to promote the act of Water Baptism is the conversion of Paul, found in the Book of the Acts of the Apostles (*Acts 9:17-18*).

Acts 9:

Verse 17 - *Then Ananias went to the house and entered it. Placing his hands on Saul, he said, "Brother Saul, Yeshua ADONAI, who appeared to you on the road as you were coming here--has sent me so that you may see again and be filled with the Holy Spirit."*

<u>Verse 18</u> - *Immediately, something like scales fell from Saul's eyes, and he could see again. He got up and was baptized...*

We must keep in mind that the same Greek word **apolouo** {ap-ol-oo'-o} used in verse 18, is the same word used for being "Washed" referring to both baptism with water and baptism in the Holy Spirit throughout the New Testament, including by such individuals as John the Baptist, Yeshua, Peter, and Paul. So, we cannot simply assume that the word "baptized" in <u>verse 18</u> refers to water baptism. It has also been established that the phrase "filled with the Holy Spirit" would have been synonymous with "baptism in the Holy Spirit." Therefore, from this chapter itself, we find strong evidence that the baptism Paul received was baptism in the Holy Spirit, not water baptism, considering there was no pool or running water in the house Paul was staying in at the time Ananias visited him.

The assumption is that <u>Verse 18</u> is recording the occurrence of both items Ananias was sent to accomplish. And there is no reason from the context to assume otherwise. So, judging from just this passage in chapter 9, we would assume Paul's baptism was not with water, but with the Holy Spirit since the Laying on of hands brought the Baptism of the Holy Spirit into Paul, and by this means, Paul Baptized Converts to Yeshua by means of the laying on of hands, and receiving the Baptism of the Holy Spirit.

A perfect example in how Paul explains this to the Church in Corinth: "And such were some of you: but you are washed (*apolouo*), but you are sanctified, but you are justified in the name of Yeshua ADONAI, and by the Spirit of our God (*1 Corinthians 6:11*).

Paul himself denounced in his Gospel of Faith, that Salvation was not through acts performed according to the Law of Moses, nor having to be converted into Judaism first by performing the act of circumcision nor baptism in water in order to show your conversion into the Law of Moses (as the Church and Apostles in Jerusalem were imposing). The Commission that Yeshua ADONAI gave to the Apostle Paul was to go and bring the Heathen Nations (the Gentiles) into the Kingdom of God, and Paul strongly denounced having to perform any act other than the submission of the individual through Faith, into receiving their Salvation through the Death and Resurrection of Yeshua ADONAI. The Laying-On of Hands after the individual received their Salvation was to receive the Baptism of The Holy Spirit and be "Washed Clean", but not through the Jewish tradition of Water Baptism in order to convert the individual into Judaism; but rather bring the individual Spiritually out of Death and Eternal Judgement into Life Eternal, so that the person may be "Born Again" as well as receive their Salvation through Faith in Yeshua ADONAI.

The manner in which the Apostle Paul was Baptized, would be the same manner in which he would Baptize and teach in regard to what Baptism was. Through his Commission by Yeshua to be the Apostle of the Gentiles, Paul would establish the World-Wide Church and the Manners of Conduct and the Rules of Engagement by which the Church (Body of Yeshua) would conduct itself as both a messenger and disciple of Faith from then and that point forward. It would become the doctrine of the Church.

In conclusion, Water Baptism is not a requirement in order to be Saved or have acceptance into the Body of Yeshua; and anyone who tells you it is, is a Liar and should be rebuked as a Reprobate. It is a self-appointed act under the mandate of individuals who feel they need a water cleansing in order to feel that they have done something which justifies their faith and symbolizes the death of the old man (being submerged), and then renewal of the new man in ADONAI (being resurrected out of the water) leaving behind the filth of their sins. This of course is not true, because our sins have already been forgiven us even before we accept Yeshua as our Lord and Saviour, but rather it is our heartfelt Faith that makes us Proclaim with our mouths, what our heart has already received, and that is that we desire our Salvation through Him and this can only be done through Faith, Faith in Yeshua ADONAI! 100% without any doubt or any act of works.

The Apostles got it wrong in the beginning when the Church in Jerusalem was being formed and was the center of the Christian Faith in the first century. The Acts of the Apostles which are recorded in a compilation of chronological events (The Book of Acts), as written by the Greek Antioch Physician (Doctor Luke), who was a convert, follower and bedside aid of the Apostle Paul, shows how in the beginning the Jerusalem Church totally conformed to the beliefs and traditions of the Jewish Torah, the Laws of Moses and the Rabbinical Traditions.

Church Patriarchs such as the Apostle Peter, the Apostle John and James the half-brother of Yeshua (who had been appointed as the Leader of the Church in Jerusalem) had fully embraced the Traditional Jewish Laws and Traditions as a requirement into membership of the Church. They strongly opposed Paul when he first visited their Assembly to pronounce what Yeshua had conveyed to him as the method and approach; he was to take in building the World-Wide Church to the Gentile Nations. They sought to destroy Paul's efforts at every place he had established Assemblies throughout Asia-Minor and Europe, by claiming conformance to the Jewish Laws and Traditions, including Circumcision and Water Baptism. Peter however, as the years went by, saw the fruit of Paul's Gospel of Faith and the successful conversion of Greek and Romans into the Gospel Message and Salvation by the thousands. John and the others followed as well and the manner in which Paul had established the Church eventually over-rode what the Church in Jerusalem had been teaching and imposing.

Nevertheless, as the context and content began to come together in the 3rd and 4th centuries to decide what would be the make-up of Gospels and additional references to the New Testament Scriptures, Canon Law and Traditions embedded themselves into that effort. After the destruction of the Temple in Jerusalem in 70 A.D. and the sacking of the Jewish Nation (ISRAEL), the development of the Church Order gave way to Religious Politics and began dividing Truth into

Legend and Mystery of Content gave way to Scholastic and Priestly interpretation. The common person could not decipher, understand nor convey the Gospel, but could only be ruled and dominated by its Laws and Obedience to the Church under the threat of condemnation by God if violated. We still see that being perpetrated to this day through many different Assemblies and Religious Orders within the Christian Church.

What the Gospel of ADONAI teaches and proclaims, is that we are all sinners and fall short of the Glory of God, and that there is no means by which we can redeem ourselves through acts or works, or atonement or law. It proclaims that God Himself has given all of us, Jew and Gentile, the Way and the ability to be redeemed and have our sins washed away and then Receive Salvation into Everlasting Life.

What the "Good News" is, is that Yeshua of Nazareth came as the Only Begotten Son of the Father, that God proclaimed Him to be the Son of God (Elohim - direct extension of the Father) and Saviour of all mankind. That our conversion from Death into Life would be through our heartfelt belief that Yeshua is the Son of God, both ADONAI (Lord) and God, and that his Sacrificial Death fulfilled and paid for all of the Atonement of mankind's sin and gave complete Propitiation of our sins Forever. It thus proclaims that His Resurrection from Death, by the Power of God the Father, completely eradicates the Spirit of Death, the Powers of Darkness and the Grave from ever being imposed through the Judgement of God on us and secures Everlasting and Eternal Life for all that receive it through Faith (*Ref: Romans 10:8-12*).

That's it folks, anything else is man-made and not part of God's Purpose.

35

Where is Justice under the Law

From Ken, who by Faith has been called by the Great God and Saviour to be a teacher and is an Elder in the Church who declares the Truth regarding Yeshua ADONAI as being the Sovereign Lord and God. May you open your eyes and your heart to the truth.

Finding the Truth from the human scheme of things through a so-called Justice System under the law, means that there are two sides, a plaintiff and a defendant, in which one is already the guilty party but is being hidden from both the judge and or a jury. It must be proven by human interaction, argument and evidence through representatives (Attorney's / Lawyers) to a jury of 12 people, who must by law do their best to prove that their side is innocent beyond a reasonable doubt, whether it is true or not. So, in many cases, the guilty may be found not guilty and go free and the reverse can be true where the innocent may be found guilty and face punishment under the law even to the extent of imposing death.

The notion that Justice reveals the Truth through the process of the Law is falsely narcissistic and evil and shows how distant we are from the order in which God derives what Truth is.

The Law was given by God to man in order to show how sinful the true nature of man really is and how difficult it would be for man to obtain righteous standing in the Presence of Absolute Holiness and Truth. It could also be said that the Law helped establish the governance of civilization and placed order to that governance, but that is not necessarily how it has turned out to be. It was, when God was the One you had to answer to, but since human beings now control that order, it has been handed over to politics and the forces of evil being able to use it as an order for itself to circumvent the truth. It has always been and will continue to be a corrupt system maintained by public officials, lawyers and attorneys and judge advocate, to use the power of the court system for their own political or personal advocacy which does not serve "We the People". Any time you have a human being sitting behind a bench wearing a robe judging another human being under the statues of the law, then corruption and injustice is without doubt instilled because of the sin factor in all humans, and you will never find the truth or a righteous outcome of judgement unflawed.

The Law does nothing but hold each and every one of us accountable to our inherent Sin Nature and constant abilities to break the statutes of the Law and become Law Breakers (Criminals), by reason of the imposing edicts according to the Law. It is an overlord of us all, "We the People".

The fact that an oath must be taken in order to hold an individual accountable to the Truth when giving a testimony, which then becomes under the Law a "Sworn Testimony" so that such a breech becomes a violation of Perjury, shows how sinister the Law characterizes our human systemic sin nature.

No matter how good you try to be or how honest and forthright your actions may be in going about your daily life, the Law is a constant overlord which insights prejudice and judges everything we do.

There is no reward under the Law, only the accepted compliance which is expected of you with it, but notwithstanding, there is punishment and condemnation if you cannot meet the "Letter Of" or the interpretive context of the Law. According to the Law, if broken or violated, you must be held accountable and bound to its power and authority. You are seen by its edicts as a Law Breaker.

Grace, Mercy and Forgiveness are not virtues which the Law expounds or perceives under its jurisdiction. Therefore, Justice is the outcome of Judgment and not the Law. The Law addresses
the condition of sin and the events of lawlessness but cannot pass Judgment.

The Law stands as witness of the sin and lawlessness and will be used as the standard by which judgment passes the measure of punishment according to the statutes prescribed within it.

Human justice is flawed in rendering a completely righteous verdict because of the influence of sin by the one who is acting as the judge; therefore, the truth cannot be completely revealed which would influence the action taken without impartiality in order to prescribe a perfect and righteous measure of punishment.

In order to have perfect judgment, the One who is acting as judge would also have to be perfect, so that no appeal could ever be filed against the judgment rendered and that the judgment would stand on the merit of its authority without the law.

Our difficulty as Human Beings has been with our struggle to obtain perfection under the Law. This, of course, was not the intent behind God giving the Law.

It was given to man under a shroud of mystery and could never be the hope of salvation that would redeem man from his sin, thus giving us perfection with God.

So, under the perspective of what Truth Is, it is not the Law, for the Law only condemns and enlightens the nature and action of God's displeasure with man because of sin, but at the same time gives man a temporary way out from total destruction by a Holy God who cannot allow sin to stand in His Presence.

Notwithstanding, if Truth is based on a secular perspective, then it is tainted by a variety of different views and equations obtained through human intellectual and interactive knowledge (ideologies and philosophies) and will have possibly many gods (deity) and the division of many religions and cult factions arise with no absolute conjecture.

No matter how you divide it, Trial by Jury, Trial by Judge or just good old negotiations and side bar deals, in the American Justice System, the winners in all of this are the Arbitrators and Lawyers. You may have the right to represent yourself, but it is highly improbable that you will be able to function as such due to all of the rules and protocols required and imposed by the Court System and the Bar Association, making it impossible for a citizen to do so. It is an Elitist Club to say the least. "We the People" see it as a very corrupt and Good Old Boys Club and a Big Money Maker for attorneys to become Super Stars and Rich. Over the years the

Judicial System has moved more and more into the Legislative by imposing themselves (Judges) as Law Makers rather than interpreting and upholding the law(s). Our systems of government are so overwhelmed by tens of thousands of laws, bureaucrats, lawyers and judges that we cannot see any part of Liberty or Justice any longer because of them. It is time to start asking God for the right thing and it's not for God to Bless America, we are way beyond that, but rather, God, **Help** America!

36

Where does the Lord God (ADONAI)
want our worship to be?

He demands that it be focused on Him and only Him!
The sinful and defiled nature of the human race wants
to focus on what it can see and feel and partake from
the five senses of our human being.

The earth is not a point of worship;
The sun and moon are not a point of worship;
The stars in the heavens are not a point of worship;
The Immaculate Conception is not a point of worship;
The human mother of Jesus, Mary is not a point of
worship, neither is Joseph, for they were both in need
of a Saviour;
Angels are not a point of worship;
Any Icon or Statue is not a point of worship, there is no
image to worship God by, for God is Spirit;
No animal is a point of worship;
No building or structure is a point of worship;
The Cross is not a point of worship;
The Empty Tomb is not a point of worship;
The Shroud of Turin is not a point of worship;
Miracles are not a point of worship;
No Prophet, Priest or pronounced holy man is a point of
worship;
No appointed Saint is a point of worship;
No Clergyman is a point of worship;
No religion is a point of worship;
"The Church" is not a point of worship;
Our children and our family are not a point of worship;

252

No musical group, celebrity, politician or any man is a point of worship, for <u>no man</u> on this earth is Holy; No book or writing is a point of worship (not even the Bible); NOTHING in the physical creation is a point of worship!

There is only <u>ONE</u> Point of Worship that the Lord God Almighty has appointed; and that is Himself! For He has proclaimed Himself to be above ALL THINGS in His Creation, in heaven and on earth, for He is Holy and Righteous to be Worshiped and demands that worship to be only unto Himself.

When God came to earth as a man (the Man God, Yeshua ADONAI-Jesus Christ-the Son of God) to give himself as a ransom for all mankind and give propitiation for all sin that mankind has and could ever commit, He was without sin and Holy. A direct representation of the Father in Heaven, the One and Only True God (YaHaVah).

For the Lord God is One (Adonai echad) To call any human or anything in the creation Holy, is blasphemy!

Be very careful where <u>YOUR</u> worship is directed to!

37

The Devil Made Me Do It

From Ken, who is an Elder in the Church, and who by Faith has been called by the Great God and Saviour, Yeshua ADONAI *(Jesus the Christ)*. I am led by the Holy Spirit (*Ruach HaKodesh*) to write you and reveal what the Lord God (*ADONAI*) is saying. The Lord God is not pleased with this Church as it is assembled in these times and in the way the True Gospel is not being conveyed.

The Spirit of God says, "*You blaspheme and insult ME when you come together in your so-called sanctuaries of worship. You are not worshiping ME as much as entertaining yourselves. I desire True Worship, Unwavering Worship, Faithful Worship and not a show. I stand in the midst of your fellowships where both the Faithful (Hot) and Unfaithful (Cold) come together. Oh, Church of Laodicea, how I wish you were either Hot or Cold, this is why I will vomit you out of my mouth because you are lukewarm. This is not your Church; it is MY Body. I AM the Sanctuary that you enter into, the sacrament that you share in; yet you are sick, broken in spirit, scared, in need of and asking for every worldly desire, unfaithful, unrepentant, bold in your sin and in fear of the Enemy, cowards with no backbone to stand against that which you fear, you should Fear ME and not MY Enemy! Too many of you enter into MY Sanctuary with doubt and very little faith, it is all a show and because of that, you will receive No Reward. Too much of the Body Assembled are being given the wrong message, a false gospel, and not worshiping ME, the Lord your God, but instead inviting and glorifying the Powers of Darkness and the Prince of Darkness into the Assembly of the Faithful and glorifying him instead of ME. Your obsession with the Devil and his power over you is quite despicable*", thus says the Lord God Almighty!

The Lord God has also given me something to say to you: That HE is slow to Anger, yet HIS Judgement shall be swift. That HIS Love is Unconditional and Forever Lasting, yet HIS Patience is coming to an end. That we (humans) were created for HIS Pleasure and HIS Purpose and HE has Commanded us to Worship only HIM and no other. That HE has given Everything to us and sacrificed everything for us in order that we may stand before HIM undenounced and sinless and righteous in our standing. HE wants our Worship, unconditionally, and will allow no rivals.

This is what the Lord God is saying, "*IAM Coming Soon and I bring MY Reward and MY Judgment with ME!* ". We (*Human Beings*) are the highest order of God's Creation, for we are all created in the image of God. We are Spirit Beings having a human experience and are the only part of the creation (*both in Heaven and the physical universe*) whereby Faith can be exercised, and therefore the act of Faith be honoured as an expression to the true Nature and Will of God the Father. Only mankind has been given the act of exercising Faith...it is the essence of an expression given by those with a "Born Again" Spirit (Renewed by Repentance) unto the Presence of God the Father

(YaHaVah). It has been given by order of God that all human creation have a free will of choice; but because of our unique position within the creation, we have been given the right of a Free Will to express Faith in any way we purpose to. Our choices and actions are our own and any consequence derived by those actions (Good or Evil) is ours alone to bear, nothing and no one makes us do anything, we act out of our own desires, either to do Good or Evil. This is even more so evident for the Believers of the Way because we know the Truth and are held accountable to it and we have the True Gospel, that, *"Our Captivity to Sin is Over!"*. We stand in assurance that through our confession of Faith, that Yeshua ADONAI is the One True God and He has died and been risen from death by God the Father (YaHaVah), thus conquering death and the World of the Dead and giving all who will believe in Him, the Forgiveness of all sin and Everlasting and Eternal Life forever and thus placing their names in the Book of the Living (Book of Life).

There is without any doubt, a very real and vile Adversary of both God and man, a Being so deprived and sinister that he is the "Epitome of Evil" and he can never receive forgiveness nor Eternal Life in the Presence of God, he and those angels that followed him are doomed to Eternal Damnation in the Lake of Fire. He is a liar, in fact Yeshua called him "the Father of Lies" (John 8:44) also rendered him as "a murderer and does not stand in the Truth". Yeshua called him by name, "Satan" or the Devil. He is a Spirit Being with great power and status among the Spirit Beings that God has Created and claims the power over the entire world that God had given to Adam before His fall from Grace through an act of disobedience and blasphemy while in the Garden of God (Eden) (Genesis chapter 3).

All of the kingdoms of this world are under his spiritual control and deception. Satan gravitates toward Good in order to bring about Chaos and confusion in the midst of Goodness. He does this by using Doubt, which is Sin. Doubt is the direct opposite of Faith and is birth by planting strong deception, turning the Truth into a Lie and a Lie into the Truth. Because he is spirit, he has the power to introduce (Temptation) of a thought into the mind of a weak individual which becomes a tempting manifestation of their flesh and act out a sinister or perverted deed which stains their soul with a sin consciousness, which then, separates them from the Will of God and any ability to Glorify and Worship Him. This is where some in this Church (Body of Christ) are being deceived and listening to defiled and lying spirits which sounds like the truth but is a lie. False teaching by false teachers messaging that we should be on the look-out because the Devil is trying to steal your soul and he will make you do things (sin) that will lead you to the Gates of Hell. Fear, Fear, Fear... It puts the message and manifests the idea that the influence of the Devil is more powerful than God and His Influence and instead of living a faithful life and strengthening your faith towards worshiping God and all of His Goodness, you maintain a sin consciousness and fear falling into Satan's temptations.

Listen! Satan cannot, nor is he trying to steal your soul for himself, you give it away by not believing the Truth and enjoy a lie because it tantalizes and excites your sinful flesh. The Devil does not occupy, nor does he control Hell and he is not trying to drag humans there. He and his defiled crew of fallen angels (demons) are free spirits roaming the earth and heaven above it. They are interested in one thing and one thing only, keeping us (humans) from the knowledge and receiving the forgiveness of our sins and Eternal Salvation which God has afforded us through Yeshua ADONAI. It's all about the control of the human element through insulting and blaspheming God and His Holiness, using us as the pawn and tool of obstruction and insurrection, by separating us from the Creator and maintaining that control; this is the total objective and passion behind the Powers of Darkness which inundates this control.

Their major goal and purpose in their damnable and useless existence is to blaspheme God by taking His Highest Order of Creation and turn us against our God and Creator and render us to be the same as he is, Damned. He uses us to slap God in the Face. He believes that he will win this battle which he wages against the Almighty God with us as his prize. This is his true character and obsession in how he is totally consumed by deception and as a liar.

This is why we are separated from God and are in need of His Salvation to bring us in good standing with Him. The key perspective for us to understand is that God is Eternal, and because of that, He is Holy. He will not allow sin to co-exist in His Presence. There is no tolerance for sin in the Abode of God. It's not love that makes us desire tolerance or co-existence with sin, it's our innate sin nature that tolerates co-existence with being disobedient to the Will of God. The Word of God says that sin flees from His Presence. It is both a spiritual battle being waged between the Powers of Darkness and the Powers of Light in High Places and between Good and Evil here

amongst us in the physical realm.

Nevertheless, this constant fear messaging glorifies the Enemy of God and spiritually gives him a stronghold over the individual and the Assembly of the Believers. The "Cop Out" for this and the soothing of the unfaithful mind is to say, "**The Devil Made Me Do It**' meaning that they had no control over their own actions and may even in a comedic way justify their sinful act and deceive them into believing it is excusable. This is an acceptable reasoning among many and a false gospel being exploited within the Church.

There is also one other false assumption of a Truth that most Christians make, and that is to say, even though God has forgiven us of all our sins by way of the Eternal Sacrifice which Yeshua gave for us, that as we continue to sin, we must repeatedly go before Him to confess those sins and keep claiming forgiveness. This is another deception that the Powers of Darkness use to keep us under a Sin Consciousness and feeling guilty, which robs us of our Liberty and Freedom that Yeshua has given. The one thing that is forgotten is that the Lord God says, "*Go and sin no more*", this is a plea for us to stop. That a constant coming before the Lord God to ask for HIS forgiveness of a repeated act of sin, shows a lack of Faith and a willfulness to keep sinning. This keeps the Child of God in disobedience and grieves the Spirit of God. In doing so, we are on the edge of HIS judgement at this point and if we cannot take control of our Faith and we become a reprobate in HIS sight, then HE will remove us from this life so that our flesh will go to the grave, along with the sin, and our spirit will stand in the Presence of the Lord, and we will sin no more. (Example: 1 Corinthians 5:5)

The Lord God has already announced to all of His Creation, to everything that has been created in the Spirit Realm of Light and those of Darkness and to us His First Born of the Physical Creation, "*That every knee shall bow and every tongue confess, that Yeshua ADONAI, Jesus is Lord, to the Glory of God the Father YaHaVah*"

But, make no mistake of it, Satan's fate is already sealed to the Lake of Fire, which has been prepared before the Foundations of the Earth, where he and his fallen angels shall spend all of Eternity, damned and in torment forever.

A Ha Vah   Ya Ha Vah
Love   Father God

GOD'S MESSAGE TO THE WORLD

THE TIME HAS COME AND IS ALREADY HERE WHEN THE LORD GOD IS DIRECTLY SPEAKING AND REACHING OUT TO HIS HIGHEST ORDER OF HIS CREATION, **WHICH IS YOU**!

IAM the Beginning and the End, the One who sits on the Throne of Heaven, the Highest Heaven, there is nothing above Me or beside Me, everything is below Me. No other deity, lord or God exists in the Creation of all things which I have Commanded into existence. IAM the Father to My Children, YaHaVah; The Great IAM, YAHWEH. To all that believe and worship Me, who know that IAM that IAM and trust in Me as their Redeemer and Saviour and call upon My Name for their Salvation and Everlasting Life in My Presence forever, I Will Forever hold on to you. I will Bless those that Bless you, and I will Curse those who come against and curse you!

IAM Spirit and IAM Holy, IAM Eternal, from Everlasting to Everlasting. IAM the only God and there is no other!

IAM the Lord God, ADONAI. IAM the Final Judge of all things and will solely determine who enters into My Kingdom or will be cast out of My Presence into the Lake of Fire Forever.

IAM Love and My Love is unconditional. All Righteousness and Justice reside with Me. IAM the One who is Truthful and Faithful in giving all things to those that Love Me and keep my Commandments.

I created everything that is seen and unseen, in Heaven and all of the physical universe which is Mine to Command at Will.

IAM the Ruler of Heaven and earth and My footstool is the earth where I have created Life of every kind and have Commanded My Spirit to engage everything that I have created and to bring forth Life in abundance for My Glory and My Purpose.

Out of all my Creation, **you** are the essence of My Kind, created in the Image of Us, Elohim, and Our Purpose, with My Spirit being given to them that was the first of my Creation. To have dominion and authority over the earth and all of the physical Creation.

Nevertheless, I have this against you.

I cursed all of your kind when at the beginning of creation your kind sinned against Me, blasphemed My Commandment that I had given to them and broke My Covenant that I made with them. Therefore, in Righteous Judgement I punished them and all their seed going forth from them. I cast them out of My Presence and removed my Spirit from within them, so that death would come upon them and you because of Sin that which they had done against Me. You shall not be able to escape from Me, nor elude Me. There is no space that I do not occupy in Heaven or in this physical universe.

My presence is felt in everything that I have Created. My Majesty is expressed to you in all that has been given and seen.

Your kind has shown Me that from your beginning, the heart and soul of your kind is set on nothing but evil and malice against Me and even unto yourselves, so much so, that I had regretted even creating your kind and wanted to put an end to all of you. Yet My Unwavering Love and Purpose for your kind overrode my wrath and anger towards you.

IAM the One who has forgiven all of your inequities and sin against Me, past, present and future. IAM the One who has redeemed you and offers you Eternal Life with Me Forever! No one else can do this for you. You worship and adore false god's, false prophets, false teachers that I have condemned and hate which you place before Me. You liars, that deceive in your religions, false narratives and false idols believing in something that does not exist, all of you shall be condemned to the Lake of Fire and separated from Me Forever!

You come from Me and in Righteousness you shall return unto Me in My Presence, but in unrighteousness you shall be cast away from My Presence and bound in everlasting darkness. IAM the One who gives you Life and Existence and this Life that I have given you I hold in My Hand for My Purpose.

You cannot save yourselves, yet you have the Power given to you in order to be Saved. IAM the One who has given you that Power. I have fulfilled all righteousness in order for you to have this Power and to receive Everlasting Life in My Presence Forever. To forgive you of all of the inequities and sin that you have perpetrated against Me.

I came to you from the Father, as the Father in the form as the Son of God, in order to announce the Good News to you, that YOUR CAPTIVITY TO SIN IS OVER! That in fulfillment of all Righteousness, I Yeshua Adonai, which is the Name above all Names, in Heaven, on earth and in the world of darkness which falls under My Judgement, have taken all of your sins against Me and forgave you of all of it; Past, Present and Future.

That in My Name I seal a New and Everlasting Covenant with you. I took your death unto Myself and rose from the Dead by the Power of the Great IAM and removed the Curse of Death from you and freely give that Power to anyone who will confess in their soul and from their heart, in Unwavering Faith that IAM, Yeshua Adonai, the Lord their God, to the Glory of the Father.

That you shall Worship Me and receive My New Covenant by which I will write your name into my Book of the Living, and on the Final Day that I will Judge everything in all of My Creation, I will Passover your Sins and welcome you into my Kingdom Forever.

IAM the Lord your God, and you were Created out of My Love and Righteousness and because of My Great Love and Mercy for you and your kind, IAM coming to you, that you may know the Truth and the conditions set forth for My Return.

IAM slow to Anger, not willing that any of you fall into the darkness and perish, but My Patience is coming to an end, and I shall not suffer you any longer and My Spirit shall no longer moan over your inequities and sins which cry out for My Wrath and Judgement to fall upon you.

Take heed and be prepared, for I come like a thief in the night and take what is truly Mine, all of you who are part of my Covenant, those I call My Children.

Behold, truly I say to you, IAM coming soon, and I bring my reward with Me for those who Love Me, but My Wrath shall stand against those who deny Me and blaspheme my Spirit with the Free Gift that I have Given unto their Salvation. This shall not be forgiven of them now and or forever.

IAM the Lord your God, there is **No Other!**